EVERY WORD

A Reader's 90-day
Guide to the Bible

SUSAN GOODWIN
JENNIFER PETERSON
MOLLY SAWYER

Cover art by Emily Fritz
Cover design by Rick Fossum

ISBN: 9781790623730

S.G. > To my husband Tom and the arrows in our quiver, Dorothy Grace and Tommy, Lily, Anna, Phoebe, and Lucy. You all have my heart and it is the joy of my life to magnify the Lord with you and exalt His name together.

J.P. > To my family and to God's glory

M.S. > To Doug, my one, and to our three — Avery, Abby, and Hayes. I have no greater joys on this earth. This is for you. May we always wonder at this love so amazing and these promises so unfailing.

CONTENTS

"Man shall not live by bread alone, but by EVERY WORD that comes from the mouth of God.**"**

—Jesus (Matthew 4:4b)

"God's way is perfect and his Word is flawless. A perfect God could have nothing less than perfect communication with his people. It is we who read hastily, skip prayer, and fail to meditate on His Word, who find it confusing.**"**

—Tim Keller (*The Songs of Jesus*)

INTRODUCTION
& how to use this guide

When was the last time you read a great novel by starting in the middle, or three-fourths of the way through? Do you revisit your favorite book by reading just one chapter over and over again? Can you get an author's message by choosing unrelated sentences from his work, piecing them together, and coming up with your own conclusion? Would you feel the true impact of an epic story if you left out the hard parts or never read the ending?

No — when you read a great narrative, you begin with the first word and read to the concluding *The end.* It's the journey through the carefully crafted elements that make the story enjoyable, powerful, and inviting. It's the only way to feel the full weight of the author's expression and intent.

The narrative of the Bible is no different. The Bible is first and foremost a beautiful love story. It is a story that is all about God. If we really want to know Him, we must know His story from beginning to end.

Several years ago, we invited a few friends to read the Bible this way with us, determined to grow in our understanding of God and His story. It was simple. We committed together that we would read through our Bibles chronologically an hour a day for the next 90 days, from "In the beginning" all the way to "forever and ever." Since that first group of readers, we have continued to gather communities of readers to journey through the Bible in 90 days.

As we read EVERY WORD of the Bible, the story begins to lift off the pages and settle in our hearts. It becomes apparent that this isn't just any story; it is THE story. "The true story of the whole world," as Michael Goheen says. As we read and wrestle through the story in faith, it also becomes apparent that it is OUR story. God graciously invites us in, not just as passive observers, but onto the very stage as participants continuing the story on to its grand conclusion. When we realize we are part of the story, everything changes.

With the help of this little book, you'll discover the grand narrative of the Bible and how to take your place in its story. Think of us as your tour guides. A good tour guide leads you around, gives you helpful information, and then steps back to allow you to experience the great sights for yourself.

This is not a Bible study where you will dig deeply into the nuances of the text. That is for the scuba divers—the patient explorers who go deep beneath the surface to experience the colors and textures of the underwater world. For the next 90 days, we are instead astronauts. High above the earth's atmosphere, we are rewarded with the majesty and beauty of the entire planet. Both scuba divers and astronauts experience the same world, but from different perspectives. Reading the whole Bible in just 90 days lets you soar over the entire story in all its splendor. We will see God's great love and His plan to rescue humanity and restore all things through His son Jesus. Grasping this big picture will give new richness to specific stories and deeper meaning to individual verses of the Bible as you return to reading like a scuba diver on day 91.

Reading the whole Bible in 90 days is a bit like training for a long-distance race. It is entirely possible even for brand-new runners, but just as for experienced runners, it requires dedication, focus, and a little sacrifice. Some of your normal activities and pastimes may need to shift in order to complete each day's reading. But we promise it's worth it.

God's words created the universe, and they can change your life. Give it a try! Get your Bible and a few friends and join us as we immerse ourselves in the living, active word of God. From walking with readers from all faith backgrounds, all ages, and all life experiences, we can say with great certainty that you will never be the same.

HOW TO USE THIS GUIDE

The EVERY WORD 90-day chronological Bible reading plan appears on pages 8 through 11 of this book. We have divided the 90 days of Bible reading into 13 weeks.

Before you read, glance at each week's *Don't Miss* page. It summarizes the main points to look for as you read, including big themes, pivotal events, and key words.

For each week, we've written just a few pages to help you better understand the reading. We've addressed common questions, and we've covered all 66 books of the Bible. Take in this text in small bits throughout the week, or perhaps all at once at the end of each week.

The timeline that runs across the bottom of every page puts major Bible events in order, to help you quickly get your bearings. We've included events and people from your reading that aren't otherwise mentioned in our text; the ones we do mention appear in bold type.

Never substitute this book for your daily Bible reading. This book is a supplement, not a replacement. Don't miss the experience of reading the Bible for yourself.

If you are reading with a group, this book can serve as a review to jump-start a discussion. Three helpful questions for group discussion or individual reflection are:

> What did you learn about God?
> What were your *Aha!* moments?
> How did this connect to the big story of the Bible?

Don't reach for this book without God's word in the other hand!

TIPS FOR SUCCESS

Bible. Choose a version, size, and format that is the most readable for you. In this guide, we'll quote from the English Standard Version, but any modern translation will do. If you are comfortable reading on an electronic device, make sure it is one suitable for long periods of distraction-free reading — probably not a smartphone.

Pray. Begin each day's reading with prayer. God wants you to know Him, and prayer helps open our hearts to hearing God through His word. "Open my eyes, that I may behold wondrous things out of your law" (Ps. 119:18) is a simple prayer that reflects a teachable heart. As you read, stop and pray when you feel stuck.

Read. The only thing you have to do here is read. This guidebook contains no questions to stop and answer, no blanks to fill in. Just read. Read carefully, read thoughtfully, and keep reading. Press through the sections that are confusing and focus on what is clear. Give yourself grace if you get behind — you probably will at some point — and get back to reading as soon as you can.

Prioritize. Plan on reading for 45 to 60 minutes each day, and guard that time as a special daily appointment. Carry your Bible with you and make use of small gaps in your day to help you stay on track or get back on track. Ask God to stave off the obstacles that may keep you from reading.

Listen. We find that listening to the text, such as with a Bible app, can help us keep our minds focused as we read along. But we don't recommend listening without following along visually. If you try listening, be honest with yourself about how much you are paying attention and how much you are getting out of it. No matter what, as you read, make sure your heart is listening to what God may have to show you in His word.

Think. Understanding and reason are the solid foundations of our faith, not its enemies. God commands us to love Him with our *mind* as well as with our heart (Matt. 22:37). The Bible requires and rewards our best thinking, and as we begin to know the Bible better, we will love it and God more.

Record. As you read, you will have questions, and you will want to stop and drill deeper in places. Although you won't have much time for these investigations during the 90 days, don't ignore them. Record these questions (there's space following page 134) and come back to them on day 91 and beyond. See our list of resources on page 128 for suggestions on where to turn.

Expect. Approach each day's reading with a sense of expectancy. Be prepared to be amazed. God promises:

"So shall my word be that goes out from my mouth;
   it shall not return to me empty,
   but it shall accomplish that which I purpose,
   and shall succeed in the thing for which I sent it.**"**

Isaiah 55:11

ᴵᴵThe law of the LORD is perfect,
 reviving the soul;
  the testimony of the LORD is sure,
   making wise the simple;
    the precepts of the LORD are right,
    rejoicing the heart;
     the commandment of the LORD is pure,
     enlightening the eyes;
      the fear of the LORD is clean,
      enduring forever;
      the rules of the LORD are true,
     and righteous altogether.
    More to be desired are they than gold,
   even much fine gold;
  sweeter also than honey
 and drippings of the honeycomb.
Moreover, by them is your servant warned;
in keeping them there is great reward.**ᴵᴵ**

Psalm 19:7–11

THE **EVERY WORD** 90-DAY

WEEK 1 *focus~who is God?*

1	☐	Genesis 1–13
2	☐	Genesis 14–24
3	☐	Genesis 25–34
4	☐	Genesis 35–45
5	☐	Genesis 46–50
	☐	Job 1–10
6	☐	Job 11–27
7	☐	Job 28–42

[handwritten notes: Beginnings, God's, creation, their identity, 3:15 redemption, first of, glimpse of who God is?, Big moses, dialog w/ God +3 friends]

WEEK 2

8	☐	Exodus 1–13
9	☐	Exodus 14–26
10	☐	Exodus 27–37
11	☐	Exodus 38–40
	☐	Numbers 7–9
	☐	Leviticus 1–6
12	☐	Leviticus 7–16
13	☐	Leviticus 17–26
14	☐	Leviticus 27
	☐	Numbers 1–6, 10–12

WEEK 3

15	☐	Numbers 13–24
16	☐	Numbers 25–36
17	☐	Deuteronomy 1–10
18	☐	Deuteronomy 11–24
19	☐	Deuteronomy 25–34
	☐	Psalm 90
20	☐	Joshua 1–13
21	☐	Joshua 14–24

WEEK 4

22	☐	Judges 1–9
23	☐	Judges 10–21
24	☐	Ruth
	☐	1 Samuel 1–10
25	☐	1 Samuel 11–21
	☐	Psalm 59
26	☐	1 Samuel 22–31
	☐	Psalms 34, 52, 54, 56–57, 142
27	☐	2 Samuel 1–12
	☐	Psalms 2, 51, 60
28	☐	2 Samuel 13–20
	☐	Psalms 3, 7, 63

BIBLE READING PLAN

WEEK 5

29 ☐ 2 Samuel 21–24
   ☐ 1 Kings 1
   ☐ Psalms 4–6, 8–9, 11–21

30 ☐ Psalms 22–32, 35–41, 53, 55, 58, 61–62, 64–70, 86, 95, 101, 103, 108–110

31 ☐ Psalms 50, 73–83, 88–89, 122, 124, 131, 133, 138–141, 143–145
   ☐ 1 Kings 2–3

32 ☐ Song of Solomon
   ☐ Proverbs 1–18

33 ☐ Proverbs 19–31
   ☐ 1 Kings 4–7

34 ☐ Psalms 72, 127
   ☐ 1 Kings 8–11
   ☐ Ecclesiastes 1–8

35 ☐ Ecclesiastes 9–12
   ☐ 1 Kings 12–19

WEEK 6

36 ☐ 1 Kings 20–22
   ☐ 2 Kings 1–6

37 ☐ 2 Kings 7–14
   ☐ Jonah
   ☐ Amos 1–2

38 ☐ Amos 3–9
   ☐ 2 Kings 15–16
   ☐ Isaiah 6–12, 28
   ☐ Micah 1–2

(Week 6 continued)

39 ☐ Hosea
   ☐ Joel
   ☐ 2 Kings 17:1–18:12
   ☐ Psalms 1, 10, 33, 42–49

40 ☐ Psalms 71, 84–85, 87
   ☐ Isaiah 1–5, 13–27

41 ☐ Micah 3–5
   ☐ Isaiah 29–39
   ☐ 2 Kings 18:13–20:21

42 ☐ Micah 6–7
   ☐ Isaiah 40–56

WEEK 7

43 ☐ Isaiah 57–66
   ☐ 2 Kings 21–23
   ☐ Nahum
   ☐ Habakkuk

44 ☐ Zephaniah
   ☐ Jeremiah 1–9

45 ☐ Jeremiah 10–20, 26, 25
   ☐ 2 Kings 24:1–5

46 ☐ Daniel 1–3
   ☐ 2 Kings 24:6–19
   ☐ Jeremiah 22–24, 27–31

47 ☐ Jeremiah 35–38, 45–49
   ☐ Ezekiel 1–4

48 ☐ Ezekiel 5–17

49 ☐ Ezekiel 18–25, 29–31
   ☐ 2 Kings 24:20–25:2
   ☐ Jeremiah 52:1–5; 39:1

WEEK 8

50 ☐ Ezekiel 26–28
    ☐ Obadiah
    ☐ Jeremiah 21, 32–34
    ☐ 2 Kings 25:3–26
    ☐ Jeremiah 52:6–27;
        39:2–41:18

51 ☐ Lamentations
    ☐ Jeremiah 42–44
    ☐ Ezekiel 32–36

52 ☐ Ezekiel 37–39
    ☐ Jeremiah 50–51;
        52:28–30
    ☐ Psalm 137
    ☐ Daniel 4
    ☐ Ezekiel 40–42

53 ☐ Ezekiel 43–48
    ☐ 2 Kings 25:27–30
    ☐ Jeremiah 52:31–34
    ☐ Daniel 5–9
    ☐ 1 Chronicles 1

54 ☐ 1 Chronicles 2–8
    ☐ 1 Chronicles 9:35–
        12:40

55 ☐ 1 Chronicles 13–29

56 ☐ 2 Chronicles 1–13

WEEK 9

57 ☐ 2 Chronicles 14–27

58 ☐ 2 Chronicles 28–36
    ☐ Ezra 1

59 ☐ Ezra 2–4:5; 4:24–5:2
    ☐ Haggai
    ☐ Zechariah

60 ☐ Daniel 10–12
    ☐ Esther
    ☐ Ezra 5:3–6:22; 4:6–23
    ☐ Ezra 7–8

61 ☐ Ezra 9–10
    ☐ Nehemiah 1–7
    ☐ 1 Chronicles 9:1–34

62 ☐ Nehemiah 8–13
    ☐ Psalms 91–94,
        96–100, 102, 104–107

63 ☐ Psalms 111–121, 123,
        125–126, 128–130,
        132, 134–136,
        146–150
    ☐ Malachi

From *Every Word: A Reader's 90-day Guide to the Bible*.
© 2019 by Susan Goodwin, Jennifer Peterson & Molly Sawyer.

WEEK 10

64 ☐ Matthew 1–9
65 ☐ Matthew 10–16
66 ☐ Matthew 17–23
67 ☐ Matthew 24–28
   ☐ Mark 1–2
68 ☐ Mark 3–9
69 ☐ Mark 10–16
70 ☐ Luke 1–6

WEEK 11

71 ☐ Luke 7–11
72 ☐ Luke 12–18
73 ☐ Luke 19–24
74 ☐ Acts 1–7
75 ☐ Acts 8:1–15:29
76 ☐ Galatians
   ☐ James
   ☐ Acts 15:30–18:4
77 ☐ 1 Thessalonians
   ☐ 2 Thessalonians
   ☐ Acts 18:5–19:20
   ☐ 1 Corinthians 1–6

WEEK 12

78 ☐ 1 Corinthians 7–16
   ☐ Acts 19:21–20:6
79 ☐ Romans 1–11
80 ☐ Romans 12–16
   ☐ 2 Corinthians 1–10
81 ☐ 2 Corinthians 11–13
   ☐ Acts 20:7–26:32
82 ☐ Acts 27–28
   ☐ Ephesians
   ☐ Colossians
83 ☐ Philemon
   ☐ Philippians
   ☐ 1 Timothy
   ☐ Titus
   ☐ 2 Timothy
84 ☐ Hebrews

WEEK 13

85 ☐ 1 Peter
   ☐ 2 Peter
   ☐ Jude
   ☐ John 1–3
86 ☐ John 4–9
87 ☐ John 10–16
88 ☐ John 17–21
   ☐ 1 John
89 ☐ 2 John
   ☐ 3 John
   ☐ Revelation 1–11
90 ☐ Revelation 12–22

WEEK 1

<<< DON'T MISS

> Make note of who is in obvious control. God is the implied King. He speaks and it happens.

> The garden is the first place God dwells with man. Any other time you see garden imagery in the Bible, recall the relationship, the intention and intimacy, for which God created man. It is the place to which God is drawing man back.

> Notice all the beginnings in the book of Genesis.

> The downward spiral in Genesis 4–11 is a devastating picture of what happens when we try to do life on our own terms apart from God.

> Chapter 12 is a hinge point in Genesis; God sets the rescue mission in motion.

> The covenants God makes with mankind are the backbone of the entire big story and we will follow them through the rest of the Bible.

> As you read Job, remember God is always just and good. Circumstances never change that truth.

"In the beginning, God created . . . .**"**

Genesis 1:1a

GENESIS begins with the most significant
statement in the Bible.

If you have ever attempted to read the Bible, these first chapters are familiar to you. But in their familiarity, we often miss the importance of the foundation that is being laid for the entire Biblical narrative.

God is the main character in this story. He is the first subject of the first verb. We are not the subject of this story; He is. In the opening paragraphs God reveals Himself as Creator, Good Father, and Almighty King.

> **The Trinity >>>** a foundational understanding that God is one Divine Being who exists in three distinct persons that are equal in power and nature: God the Father, God the Son (Jesus), and God the Holy Spirit. Each person of the triune God is eternal—always was, is, and will be. Each was instrumental in creation, hence God's statement "Let us" in Genesis 1:26.

The word *genesis* means *beginnings,* and in Genesis we learn the beginning of everything—except God. God was before all things, above all things, and the cause of all things. That's where our belief begins and where all of our faith holds. We are not told when creation took place, nor are we informed how it took place other than by God's powerful, life-giving word. God spoke, it happened, and because God is good, it was *good*.

>>> In ancient times, there were images of gods everywhere. Genesis taught God's people the countercultural message that God could not be reduced to a single image, that they themselves were to be the "image"! This gives worth and dignity to every single human soul created in the *imago Dei*, the image of God.

Then God did something to make it *very good*: He created man and woman. As the crown and delight of the King's creation, only the man and woman are said to bear His image (Gen. 1:27). As image bearers, Adam and Eve were God's representatives here on earth. And so are all humans. As if a mirror hangs around our necks, we are created to reflect who God is and to be ushers of His presence in the way we think, talk, act, love, serve, and forgive.

Eden, a beautiful, perfect garden kingdom, was Adam and Eve's home. Not only did God give them a home, He gave them a purpose and a mission: to fill the earth and to subdue it (Gen. 1:28). In other words, they were to extend the blessings of Eden to all the earth. This remains our mission as image bearers: Flourish. Multiply. Work. Advance the earth's potential. Make it productive. Create good for God's glory.

God's kingdom was full of His presence, beauty, order, and satisfying work. Everything thrived! And God lived with His people. All of Eden was for Adam and Eve's enjoyment with one exception, the tree of the knowledge of good and evil.

With that tree, God gave Adam and Eve the dignity of choice. They could choose obedience and allegiance to His kingdom, or disobedience and allegiance to the kingdom of self. The enemy Satan entered the garden and questioned God's word, asking, "Did God actually say . . . ?" (Gen. 3:1). Satan's tactics have not changed; he is always questioning and confusing God's word.

Adam and Eve chose to doubt God, His goodness, and His plan for their lives. They disobeyed Him. At that moment, everything changed. Shame, sin, separation, hiding, and death entered the world. The world, as God created it, was now broken. And we are only a few pages in to the story!

Nothing tainted by sin can exist in or withstand God's holy presence—so pure, so good, so consuming. Therefore, mankind must be separated from God, and Adam and Eve are driven from the garden.

The story could end here, but God's grace always exceeds man's failure. So the story continues . . . .

God did not respond to His creation in anger, but with a promise of grace and mercy. Genesis 3:15 holds the first great promise that God will restore all things. Ad-

←———————•————————•————————————————

   Mankind sins   Cast out of Eden

am and Eve's offspring will one day crush the head of the enemy. This is the promise of Jesus the Messiah! His death on the cross and resurrection will defeat Satan and the power of sin and death forever. Restoring humanity and all creation back to the beauty, flourishing, and intimacy of Eden is the great story of the Bible. Expectantly watch it unfold from this first promise.

Graciously, God dealt with Adam and Eve's sin by killing an animal to clothe them with skins (Gen. 3:21). This first blood sacrifice — the death of an innocent substitute instead of the guilty wrongdoer — also points to the cross. It provides a blueprint for dealing with sin that God's people will follow throughout the Old Testament.

The next chapters chronicle life outside the garden under the curse of sin. Struggle instead of flourishing. Jealousy, injustice, and murder instead of peace and harmony. Corruption and violence become so complete that the evil must be purged. God plans to bring a flood of waters on the earth to judge sin. To rescue a remnant from His judgment, God chooses Noah, who was "blameless" and "walked with God" (Gen. 6:9), to build an ark. After the flood, God charges Noah with the same mission He gave Adam and Eve. And He makes His second great promise, or covenant: He will never again destroy His creation with a flood, and mankind will flourish (9:1–11). As a reminder of this promise He sets the rainbow in the clouds.

Noah   The flood   The rainbow   The Tower of Babel

> **Covenant >>>** a binding agreement made in the context of a relationship between two or more people. A covenant may be unconditional or conditional ("If you do X, I will do Y"). Throughout the Bible, we'll see several important covenants that God makes with mankind. He binds Himself in love to those who will covenant with Him.

Chapter 12 unlocks more important information about God's redemptive plan. The promises God makes to Abram (later renamed Abraham) are key to understanding the rest of the story. God chooses Abram's family to be the channel for blessing and rescuing the whole world. God promises Abram that his family will become a great nation, inherit the land of Canaan, and bless the whole world (Gen. 12:2–3). That blessing would ultimately come through the death of his descendant Jesus for the sins of the world.

> **But God >>>** Anytime you see the phrase "but God" it points to His redemptive work! It indicates He is doing something we cannot do for ourselves.

God reaffirms this covenant to Abraham's son Isaac (Gen. 26:24) and to Isaac's son Jacob (35:10–12), whom He renames Israel, the name by which the family and nation will be known. What a dysfunctional family! Their failures throughout the rest of Genesis contrast with God's faithfulness. There is no situation so dire that God cannot redeem it. Even the treachery of Jacob's sons against their brother Joseph (chapter 37) becomes the salvation of their whole family (chapter 47).

← ──•────────•──────────•──────────•────────

Abram & Sarai   Sodom & Gomorrah   **Abrahamic covenant**   Hagar & Ishmael

Genesis 50:20 is not only a concluding statement for Joseph's story, but the entire book of Genesis and man's repeated failure: "As for you, you meant evil against me, but God meant it for good, to bring it about that many people should be kept alive, as they are today." The God of Abraham, Isaac, and Jacob keeps turning evil into good according to *His* plans.

>>> HOW DID WE GET THE OLD TESTAMENT?

If the Bible was written by more than 40 authors over 2,000 years, who decided what would be in the Bible?

With respect to the Old Testament, God supernaturally led the Jewish people, over time, to collect the texts that contained His word. That process took from around 2000 BC to 200 BC. The Jewish historian Josephus explained that the books we know as the Old Testament were revered by the Jews because it was self-evident that they contained the word of God. (Jews then as well as now group the same books slightly differently, resulting in a total of 24 books instead of 39.)

Jesus Himself ratified the Old Testament collections of law, writings, and prophecy as He claimed to be their fulfillment (Luke 24:44), and He quoted the Old Testament as authoritative throughout His ministry. If it's good enough for Jesus, it's good enough for us.

In contrast to the book's glorious beginning, Genesis literally ends with a coffin (50:26). God's people still awaited the fulfilment of His promises. We must read on to next week to see those plans be accomplished.

Isaac   Jacob & Esau   Joseph

JOB comes next because he was likely a contemporary of Abraham, making the book of Job a very ancient piece of literature. It is found among the books of poetry and wisdom (see page 53) and consists of narrative mixed with Hebrew poetry.

The book of Job centers on the age-old questions:

> Is God wise and just?
> Can we trust Him?
> Why do the righteous suffer?

It can be disturbing, confusing. It is a book that takes time to understand. It is one to keep coming back to!

The writer of Job bookends the story with God Himself affirming Job's righteousness. God tells us three times within the first 25 verses that Job, like Noah, is "blameless"—not that he is perfect, but that he lives his life with integrity and trusts God. In the final verses, God in rebuking Job's friends affirms Job: "For you have not spoken of me what is right, as my servant Job has" (42:7b). Keep this in mind as you read. Throughout the book, Job rightly maintains his innocence. Job never curses God, but his mistake is that he believes he is able to stand before God. In the end, he must repent of this because no man can stand before our holy God without the covering of Jesus's righteousness.

In chapters 4 through 25, Job's three friends offer a dangerous mixture of truth, half-truth, and untruth. (Any time you hear a quote from Job, check who is saying it!) Job's friends insist that he has done something to deserve his suffering. They say God is fair and just, but they have a very simplistic view of God. To them, God can be predicted and controlled with a formula: "If I am good, then God is obligated to be good to me."

Another of Job's friends' faulty theology regarding suffering is the mindset that "I must have done something to deserve this." The truth is that a world based on karma has no room for grace. However, if undeserved suffering can exist, then *so can undeserved grace*. And that is what the Bible is all about — amazing grace!

When God finally answers Job, beginning in chapter 38, He answers all of Job's questions *with Himself*. Job doesn't get the answer to "why," but he gets the answer of "Who." God Himself! Job's response, "I had heard of you . . . but now my eye sees you" (42:5), is the response of every sufferer who chooses to put his pain in God's hands and trust His goodness and wisdom. When we experience God's infinite greatness, our agony can become "light momentary affliction" in light of His "eternal weight of glory" (2 Cor. 4:17).

In the end, we see the accusing enemy Satan limited, as he always is throughout the Bible, foreshadowing his final crushing. We see our broken, sinful world filled with suffering, both deserved and undeserved. We see God as sovereign, just, good, and trustworthy in His management of earthly affairs, with reasons for everything beyond our fathoming. Finally, we see Job's undeserved suffering pointing us to the cross where Another suffered undeservedly.

WEEK 2

8	☐	Exodus 1–13	*12*	☐	Leviticus 7–16	
9	☐	Exodus 14–26	*13*	☐	Leviticus 17–26	
10	☐	Exodus 27–37	*14*	☐	Leviticus 27	
11	☐	Exodus 38–40		☐	Numbers 1–6, 10–12	
	☐	Numbers 7–9				
	☐	Leviticus 1–6				

DON'T MISS >>>

> Look for ways the Abrahamic covenant is being fulfilled.

> Notice God always establishes relationship before giving the law. This is a pattern for the gospel.

> Read the laws not from your own perspective but with your eyes focused on God's holiness, justice, and mercy.

> The tabernacle is a big deal! Separation remains but God will dwell with sinful men despite their sinfulness.

> Pay close attention to Leviticus 16, the Day of Atonement. Consider the similarities to Jesus's sacrifice on the cross.

←————————————————————•————————————————

Israelites in slavery

"You shall be to me a kingdom of priests
and a holy nation.**"**

Exodus 19:6a

EXODUS picks up the story of God's people
four hundred years after the end of Genesis. Remember,
Genesis closed with the anticipation of the unfulfilled
promises of God. His chosen people are far from being
a great nation and they are living far from the land He
has promised. Abraham's descendants are becoming as
numerous as the stars (see Gen. 15:5)—but they are
slaves in a foreign land (Exod. 1:13). This book tells of
their miraculous exodus, or departure, from Egypt and
their formation into a holy nation.

God has not forgotten His covenant with Abraham,
Isaac, and Jacob. He intends to rescue this people in order to display His glory and goodness to the whole
world. In Exodus He reveals Himself more fully, even
giving His personal name, I AM WHO I AM (Exod.
3:24). Again and again, God makes Himself *known* to
this people.

God does this through two key events in Exodus.

First, God rescues His people from slavery. The people
do not lift a finger as God frees them and plunders the
mighty nation of Egypt. God sends plagues to loosen

Moses born

the pharaoh's grip on His people and demonstrate His power over the pagan gods of Egypt. For the tenth and final plague (Exod. 12), God sends death on the firstborn of every household.

Torah >>> the first five books of the Hebrew Bible: Genesis, Exodus, Leviticus, Numbers, and Deuteronomy. These "books of Moses" are also called the Pentateuch, meaning *five scrolls*. David is referring to these five books when he writes, "The law of the LORD is perfect, reviving the soul" (Ps. 19:7a). The Hebrew word *Torah* literally means *teaching* and is often translated *law*, since these books are filled with the laws God gave the nation of Israel.

But the first list of laws does not come until 70 chapters in to the Torah—Exodus 20. The first 69 chapters of the Torah are narrative, stories of God pouring out His love on mankind. Notice, He chooses and rescues a people first. Only after that does He show them how to obey. That pattern has not changed: first God saves us by grace through faith, and then we respond with a life of obedience.

The Torah is the foundation for understanding the rest of the Bible, as the rest of the Bible's human authors assume you know the Torah already. As we read on, we will keep referring back to God's design in creation, His rescue of Israel, and His desire for a relationship with all mankind.

But God always makes a way for salvation. To live, each family was instructed to kill an unblemished lamb

← ●————————————————————————●

Ten plagues   Passover

and paint its blood on their door frame. That perfect lamb would be a substitution, dying in place of the firstborn. When God's people demonstrated their trust by carrying out this sacrifice, God's judgment *passed over* their houses. This Passover was to become an annual celebration of God's deliverance, pointing forward to the death of Jesus: "Behold, the Lamb of God, who takes away the sin of the world!" (John 1:29b).

>>> Notice when God brings people through or out of water. It is a symbol that God is moving His plan along, bringing order, giving a mission, or transforming. We see it in creation, the flood, baby Moses in the river, the Israelites through the Red Sea and across the Jordan River, Jesus's baptism, and Christian baptism today.

Second, God gathers His people at Mount Sinai to give them the laws that will teach them how to live with Him. Through His chosen leader Moses, God uses these two events to institute another covenant: the Mosaic covenant. God will bless His chosen nation as long as they obey His laws. It is this nation, God's "treasured possession among all peoples" (Exod. 19:5), who will be "a kingdom of priests" (19:6) through which God will invite the whole world to know Him.

Note that God *redeems* the people *first*. He invites and establishes *relationship first*. Then the law is given. This is a pattern we will follow throughout the Bible. The law explains how this relationship must work.

> **Redeem** >>> to buy back, such as paying a ransom to free a captive. Notice, the rightful owner is the one doing the buying. Consider how much God values us if He is willing to pay dearly for something that was already His!

For the rest of Exodus and all of Leviticus, the Israelites camp near the mountain and God begins giving the law through Moses. Great portions of Numbers and Deuteronomy are also laws. Why so many laws? (613, to be exact!) God in His awesome holiness cannot be near anything unholy or impure. Just like paper cannot occupy the same space as fire, sinful man would be consumed in the direct presence of Holy God. It is downright dangerous to come near God in an impure state. By giving the law, God lays out a way for Israel to be pure and to draw near to Him safely.

> >>> In contrast to the frenetic cultic practices of the nations around them, God's law provided security for His people. They did not have to wonder if their sacrifices would please Him. They would know on exactly what terms to approach Him with confidence.

The laws that begin in Exodus 20 can be broadly categorized as (1) timeless moral laws, (2) ceremonial laws concerning ritual purity and animal sacrifice, and (3) civil laws involving economic conduct and social justice. To live by these laws would make the nation of Israel stand out as distinctly different from the nations surrounding them. For this reason, they were not to intermarry with and adopt the customs of the surrounding nations. They were set apart to reflect their holy, just, and merciful God.

A word of advice when reading the laws: Read with your focus on God's holiness, justice, and mercy. Our modern eyes can be blind to the law's original purpose: to set Israel apart from the surrounding nations as holy. Notice that the law reveals how sin infiltrates every aspect of our lives, and shows our need for a Savior. As Paul realized 1500 years later, "Therefore the law was our tutor to bring us to Christ" (Gal. 3:24a NKJV).

Sin >>> saying no to God by living in rebellion to His rule and reign.

In addition to the laws, God gives Moses very specific blueprints to build the tabernacle. We recognize the importance of this structure, not only because there are two lengthy accounts in Exodus (chapters 25–30 and 36–40), but because this is the first time since Eden that God is making a way to *physically* dwell with man on earth. The instructions come from God, a reminder that humanity must come to God on His terms. The tabernacle is a fully portable structure that the priests will reassemble at each stop along the way to the promised land. Much of the design and decor within the tabernacle is garden-themed, reminiscent of Eden.

The tabernacle contained the ark of the covenant—the symbol of God's personal holy presence. Covered by a "mercy seat," the ark was kept behind a thick curtain

The law given   The golden calf

(veil) in the innermost room, the Most Holy Place, into which only the high priest could enter.

As Moses and the people were careful to build the tabernacle just as God had instructed, God came to live among them. "Then the cloud covered the tent of meeting, and the glory of the LORD filled the tabernacle" (Exod. 40:34). Imagine! The reality of the awesome nature of God's presence draws Exodus to a close on the sobering note that not even Moses, God's chosen leader, can enter the tabernacle when it is filled with the glorious presence of God (40:35).

LEVITICUS continues the story of God birthing a nation. The people are physically set apart; God now begins the process of spiritually setting them apart. The great deliverance of Exodus would be incomplete without Leviticus. Because the details are strange to our modern ears, this book often becomes the graveyard of well-intentioned plans to read through the Bible. Keep reading with an eye on the nature of God's holiness, and His desire to live in relationship with sinful man.

The book's title refers to its descriptions of the duties of the Levitical priests (descendants of Israel's son Levi) in the tabernacle. A priest serves as a human mediator between people and God, because sinful people cannot approach a holy God. Israel's priests were charged with the solemn responsibility of atoning for the people's sins by blood sacrifice (Lev. 1-10) so that they could continue to live in God's presence. God inviting man near was a revolutionary idea for the original readers.

←————————————•————————————

The tabernacle

The annual Day of Atonement described in Leviticus 16 was the one time each year the high priest could pass through the tabernacle's veil to where God's presence dwelled. The sacrifices offered that day would cover all the people's sins for another year. The blood of one bull and one goat must be shed, and the scapegoat must symbolically carry the people's sins far away from the camp. These sacrifices were bloody, messy reminders of the cost of sin, for sin literally destroys life (Rom. 6:23).

Atonement >>> literally, *covering over*. In the Old Testament, atonement refers to the way God's priests would cover the people's sins in God's eyes through animal sacrifices.

Yet the Day of Atonement must have felt like an outpouring of God's love, a rescuing from the weight of sin. It was a day the slate was wiped clean . . . at least for another year. The people must have longed for a day when they could enter into God's presence freely and permanently. In this way, the Levitical priests point us to Jesus, His once-for-all sacrifice and His eternal, perfect priesthood (Heb. 7:24–27)!

NUMBERS is so titled because of the census that opens it, but its original Hebrew title means "in the wilderness." With God in their midst leading them, the people were ready to move through the wilderness toward inheriting the land of Canaan.

The detailed instructions for building the tabernacle have been followed and God is dwelling where He longs to be in the midst of the people He loves, for the first time since the garden of Eden. The people are camped with God literally at their center in the tabernacle. They are organized by family, or *tribe* (Num. 2). The twelve tribes are descended from the twelve sons of Israel (Jacob). These tribes will inherit land once they get to the home God has promised them in Canaan. To honor Joseph for his part in saving the family from famine, Israel granted a double blessing by making Joseph's tribe into two, named for his sons Ephraim and Manasseh (Gen. 48). Levi will not be counted in the inheritance of land; this family will be priests in the tabernacle, with God as their inheritance (Deut. 10:9).

Feasts >>> God gave the Israelites special celebrations, including the three annual feasts of Passover, the Feast of Weeks (Pentecost), and the Feast of Booths (Lev. 23). These were woven throughout the Jewish calendar as a time of remembrance and worship for God's past faithfulness, while pointing forward to the hope of complete fulfillment in the coming of the promised Messiah.

This picture of God's people camped around the tabernacle foreshadows God dwelling with mankind through Jesus physically (John 1:14) and spiritually (Eph. 3:17), and points forward to the eternal dwelling of God with man in the new heaven and earth (Rev. 21:3). For Israel, God is present in the cloud by day and the fire by night as He leads them in the wilderness.

← ————————————————————•————————————————————

The 12 tribes of Israel

This week's reading began with God's people far from the promised land living in slavery; it ends with them dwelling in the presence of God, positioned to enter the land! What a journey! They have been saved, but their journey toward holiness and the blessings of obedience is only just beginning . . . just like us. Our personal relationship with God begins with salvation but is a continuing journey as we learn those personal lessons in holiness and obedience that lead to life and blessing.

Forming the nation of Israel

WEEK 3

DON'T MISS >>>

> This week you will spend forty years in the wilderness with the Israelites. Reflect on why a two-week road trip to the promised land turns into a forty-year desert wandering.

> Numbers is structured with sections of laws followed by stories of faithless mutiny. It highlights the rebelliousness of man's heart.

> Once we get to Deuteronomy, the new generation of Israelites is again poised to enter the promised land. Here Moses reiterates the law and gives a series of sermons spurring the people to be faithful to the covenant.

> Joshua is the exciting, hopeful, and long-awaited moment of the story in which the people finally enter the promised land!

"Not one word has failed of all the good things that the LORD your God promised concerning you.**"**

Joshua 23:14b

NUMBERS resumes at an exciting moment.

The people are on the brink of possessing a land for themselves, inheriting what God has promised! They are poised to be a kingdom of priests and a blessing to the nations.

In this action-packed book, we see the faithfulness of God met at every turn by the unfaithfulness of His people. God is dwelling in their midst; He is a cloud of shade and protection by day, a warm fire at night. He is sustaining them with the provision of manna for food each day. But there is a big problem! The people's hearts remain in the familiar state of rebellion against God, His love, and the life He offers them. In the same way, our tendency is to look for life apart from God. We try to put ourselves in His rightful place—that's pride. Or we listen to the lies of the enemy Satan—that's fear.

When Moses sends one man from each of the twelve tribes to spy out the promised land of Canaan (Num. 13), the people choose fear instead of faith. The spies report that the land is as good as God promised, yet ten of the spies evoke terror with reports of giants in the

The 12 spies   The land of milk & honey

land. Two of the spies, Joshua and Caleb, stand firm on the faithfulness of God.

The people rebel, forgetting the certain promises of God. God intervenes and forgives, but He gives the people what they want. The generation that witnessed the deliverance of the Passover and walked on dry land through the Red Sea would not live to inherit the promised land. (May we be quick to remember the faithfulness of God in our lives!) That entire generation of faithless adults will die in the desert over the next forty years. Joshua and Caleb, the two faithful spies, will then continue the journey to Canaan.

>>> Unlike many other religious texts, the Bible doesn't shy away from its characters' failings. The Bible teaches that all—even Moses—have sinned and fall short of the glory of God (Rom 3:23). Moses has been a great hero, but his failure points us to our need for a perfect hero, mediator, and savior: Jesus.

By Numbers 20, those forty years are coming to an end and the new generation is ready to move forward. But their hearts remain unchanged. They complain about the lack of water, just like their parents did, and once again God provides water from a rock through Moses and Aaron. This time, though, Moses and Aaron fail to honor God in the miracle, instead taking the credit for themselves. As a result, even these faithful leaders will not enter the promised land with God's people.

←————————•————————————————•————————

Rebellion   40 years of desert wandering

Grumbling has become a pattern for the people, so it's no surprise that they are grumbling again in Numbers 21. And, yet again, God's character is displayed in both justice and mercy. In justice, God sends poisonous snakes into the camp, and in mercy, God provides a rescue. God tells Moses to make a bronze snake and mount it on a pole. Those who look up in faith at the snake, the symbol of their destruction, will be saved. This strange story points us to Jesus. He too will be lifted up on the cross, like that bronze snake (John 3:14–15). When we look up to Him in faith and repentance, God saves us—eternally!

Reviewing Israel's unfaithfulness in the wilderness, Paul later wrote, "Now these things took place as examples for us, that we might not desire evil as they did" (1 Cor. 10:6). Just like Israel, our hearts naturally forget, responding in faithlessness and becoming hard toward God. Just like Israel, we need continual reminders of God's goodness, holiness, and His ways that lead to life.

DEUTERONOMY pauses the action as
Moses delivers a series of sermons and songs to prepare the new generation for life in the promised land as the people of God. Deuteronomy literally means *second law*. It is the most quoted book throughout the rest of the Bible. (Jesus quoted Deuteronomy when tempted by Satan in the desert.) If you have read up to this point, much of Deuteronomy will seem familiar to you. In addition to reviewing the law, Moses reminds the people of God's love that rescued and sustained them. And he

offers them a choice: love and obey God and be blessed, or rebel and disobey and be cursed.

>>> WHY IS THE LAW SO CRUEL?

Actually, it's not! Modern culture tends to view the Torah as outdated and unforgiving, but people who actually read it realize that it provides the framework for a society built on justice, fairness, and mercy.

The Torah's protections for the accused, the poor, women, and foreigners were unheard of in the ancient world. Take the famous rule of "an eye for an eye" (Lev. 24:19–20). Now think of it as a limiting principle that restricted vengeance against offenders. The alternative in other cultures would have been "I kill your whole family for an eye" if you were poorer or less powerful than your victim. By contrast, God gives rules that are to apply evenly and across economic and ethnic lines and that clearly show the intrinsic value of all human life.

The law contains protections for the accused that set the stage for modern legal systems. For example, Deuteronomy 17 prescribes a judicial process that requires a public trial and multiple witnesses. Numbers 5 provides that a woman accused of adultery be allowed to face her accuser in public and have a chance to be exonerated. Deuteronomy 19 criminalizes perjury and provides cities of refuge to protect accidental manslaughterers from criminal punishment.

Moses's sermon has become part of the great prayer in Judaism, the *Shema*. "Hear, O Israel: The LORD our God, the LORD is one. You shall love the LORD your God with all your heart and with all your soul and with all your might" (Deut. 6:4-5). This beautiful prayer emphasizes that love and relationship with God is the heart of the law. Jesus affirms this passage as the most important commandment (Mark 12:28-30). If the people follow all that God has taught them in the Torah, they will point the world to Him and His wisdom, love, and justice. They will flourish in the abundance of His blessing.

Nonetheless, God knows that the people will fail to obey Him and will experience the curses. God is faithful to all of His promises, both to bless and to curse. Moses reminds them that God is driving out the pagan Canaanite nations because of their wickedness (Gen. 15:16), not because of Israel's righteousness. After all, Israel is "a stubborn people" (Deut. 9:4-6). But God promises to rescue His people when they choose to return to Him (Deut. 30). He promises to fix their faulty hearts in a way that they cannot do themselves. After all, their—and our—greatest threat to a relationship with God comes from within, from the heart.

Moses concludes by summing up God's law: "For it is no empty word for you, but your very life" (Deut. 32:47). He pleads with the people to "choose life" (30:19). In response, the people eagerly renew their conditional covenant with God. They are now ready to enter the promised land. In the promised land they are to live as a holy nation, a nation of priests, reflecting who God is to the nations around them.

Spiritual preparation to enter the land

Though Moses will not lead the people into the land, he assures them with the reality, "The LORD your God himself will go over before you" (Deut. 31:3a). In Moses, we have a picture of the richness of a life of obedience. God says of Moses, "And there has not arisen a prophet since in Israel like Moses, whom the LORD knew face to face" (34:10). Yet Moses is mortal, and his death in chapter 34 poignantly reminds us that a greater Mediator "whom the LORD knew face to face" is still to come.

This completes the Torah, the first major section of the Bible. God has laid the foundation of the purpose and calling of this new nation. He is blessing them to be a blessing to the whole world. Joshua begins the books of history, which record how the Israelites lived out this divine calling.

>>> The twelve books of **history** in the Old Testament are Joshua through Esther. Their events happen in real time and real historical places. Their stories are often troubling. Read outside of the context of the larger narrative, they can leave us questioning God's methods. But we are to read these histories through the lens of the foundational principles of the Torah, never losing sight of God's ideals and His faithfulness to His redemptive plan.

JOSHUA chronicles the fifteen-year conquest of the land of Canaan. Joshua is the new leader following Moses's death, and his task is to drive out the wicked Canaanite nations and take possession of the land.

←————————•————————————•————————————————•————

| Moses dies | Joshua | Crossing the Jordan River |

Those of us who have received salvation through faith in Jesus are in a similar position. Salvation is ours, but there is still "driving out" to be done in our lives. We must continuously work with God to drive out our self-will, our selfish tendencies, and our sinful habits so that we may take possession of a life of blessing lived with and for Him.

Joshua >>> literally, *The LORD is Salvation* (see Num. 13:16). The Greek version of this name is Jesus! Both names describe the work God will do through these two.

Realize that God's heart is not set against the Canaanites; rather, God's heart is set against sin. *Anyone* who will turn their hearts to Him can be brought in and called His child. This is Rahab's story in Joshua 2. Her profession of faith in the God of Israel saves her family from the destruction of Jericho. She joins God's family and becomes an ancestor of the kings, including Jesus (Matt. 1:5)!

The Israelites miraculously enter the land with God's presence leading them on dry land through the Jordan River (Josh. 3–4). After many battles, the pagan Canaanite nations are conquered and the land is equitably divided among the tribes of Israel. God has made good on His promises: not one word has failed, not one of all their enemies has withstood them, and the Lord has given them rest on every side (chapter 23). The people reaffirm their commitment to God (24:16–18), and there is peace for a generation. What a remarkable journey!

The promised land   Rahab   Battle of Jericho

WEEK 4

DON'T MISS >>>

> In the dark days of the judges, notice the contrast of God's faithfulness to the people's repeated unfaithfulness.

> Ruth is a bright spot in the time of the judges. See how God brings a Canaanite woman into the family of God. Notice that there is nothing explicitly supernatural about this book; this is the story of everyday people faithfully following God's law. Peace, provision, and restoration are the by-products of obedience to God.

> Prepare for drama. In 1 Samuel, Israel gets its first human king, Saul . . . and then its second, David.

> Worship and prayerfully wrestle with God through the psalms of David.

> God describes David as "a man after his own heart." Consider what that means as you read through David's successes and failures.

←————————•————————

Settled in the land

"They have rejected me from being king over them.**"**

1 Samuel 8:7b

JUDGES recounts the next three or four hundred years of Israel's history in a not-strictly-chronological narrative. After the victories in Joshua, and a resounding affirmation of the people to follow God (Josh. 24), Judges turns to the dark side of a people who are bent on doing what is right in their own eyes.

The judges were military and judicial leaders appointed by God to rescue Israel. Judges 2:11–23 is a preview for the rest of the book: Israel would forsake God and worship idols, and God would allow the people to be defeated by their enemies. Then they would cry out, and God would send a judge to rescue them and drive out their enemies. The people would serve God as long as the judge lived, but after his or her death, the cycle of disobedience would repeat.

This cycle occurs at least twelve times in the first 16 chapters. Some of the judges, such as Gideon (chapters 6–8), Jephthah (chapter 11), and Samson (chapters 14–16), are deeply flawed characters who show that God can use anyone to accomplish His plans. Encouraging!

Judges ends with the strange stories of Micah's idols (chapters 17–18) and a Levite and his concubine (chap-

---

Gideon   Jephthah   Samson

ters 19–21). Morally and spiritually, things are out of control. Culturally, the treatment of women has degraded to an astonishing degree. God's people have abandoned the goodness of God's law, and instead of being a people distinctly reflecting who God is, they have become just like the idolatrous nations. The book's conclusion, "Everyone did what was right in his own eyes" (Judg. 21:25), underscores the hopelessness of a life lived without regard for God.

>>> Why doesn't the Bible condemn these horrible stories?

Because it doesn't need to. Don't hold your breath waiting for a clearly stated "moral" at the end of every Bible story. Remember, the authors assume you know the Torah: how things were meant to be and what God's laws say about how people should live. Don't assume that God approves something just because it was culturally "normal" or because it made it into the Bible.

We don't expect the hero of an epic war film to turn to the camera and announce, "War is awful." It would be unnecessary and detract from the dramatic impact of the movie. Just as we are meant to understand the moral of that kind of story, so too should we apply our understanding of God to the difficult stories of Judges.

For example, Jephthah made a vow to God that resulted in him offering his daughter as a sacrifice. But we know from the Torah (Lev. 20:2–5) that God condemns child sacrifice. Judges is showing us that even the leaders of Israel have begun to treat God like a Canaanite god who requires child sacrifice and never offers grace.

$\longleftarrow$ •

Judges rule

Who is Boaz's mother?

RUTH is a story of love, self-denial, and faith set

in "the days when judges ruled" (Ruth 1:1). It is a reminder that in the midst of chaos and rebellion, the faithful will be honored by God. In chapter 1, Naomi's family disobeys God by fleeing the land and intermarrying with the pagan Moabites, but in God's mercy, the ending here will be happy and hopeful.

Naomi's Moabite daughter-in-law Ruth chooses to return to Israel with Naomi. Like Rahab (Josh. 2), Ruth is brought into God's family through her faith (Ruth 1:16). She then meets Boaz, a man who knows and obeys God's laws (see Lev. 19:9–10, 25:23–25). Ruth is redeemed when Boaz agrees to buy back Naomi's property and marry Ruth, who receives all the rights and privileges of being part of his family. Remarkably, these unlikeliest of women are listed in the royal genealogy of Jesus in Matthew 1, reminding us that God's heart is for the whole world.

Redeemer >>> one who buys back or avenges. Jesus is our Redeemer in both senses. His blood bought us back from our slavery to sin, and God's righteous anger against our sin was avenged through His death. Through this redemption we are given all the rights and privileges of being part of God's family.

---

1 SAMUEL begins with the birth of the last

judge, Samuel. His mother Hannah's prayer of thanksgiving in chapter 2 introduces the themes of the rest of the book: God opposes the proud and lifts up the hum-

---

| Ruth & Naomi | Boaz | Samuel |

ble. God is at work despite human evil. And one day He will send a perfect, mighty King.

By chapter 8, the people have tired of Samuel's rule and demand a king to rule them "like all the nations" (1 Sam. 8:5). But they are really rejecting God's kingship and their calling to be a holy and distinct people who show the world what God is like. (He was not surprised by this rejection; remember that He foresaw and planned for it in Deut. 17:14–20.) This begins a five-hundred-year period of the kings of Israel.

So God gives the people a king after *their* heart. Saul is tall, strong, and handsome (1 Sam. 9:2), everything that a king should look like. And God is with Him, granting him military success and the loyalty of the people. But when Saul's pride and impulsiveness lead him to offer an unauthorized sacrifice (13:8) and disobey God's clear command (15:23), God rejects him as king. Although Saul continues to reign throughout his lifetime, his descendants will not become an enduring dynasty.

>>> Jacob gave a blessing to each of his twelve sons. Over Judah he spoke a kingly promise that "the scepter shall not depart from Judah" (Gen. 49:10), meaning that a descendant of Judah would rule an eternal kingdom. Your ears should perk up when you learn that David is from the tribe of Judah (1 Sam. 17:12). God's plan is in play! In Revelation it all comes together when we read that Jesus, "the Lion of the tribe of Judah, the Root of David, has conquered" (Rev. 5:5).

← ———————•———————————•——————————

Israel gets a king   Saul

Meanwhile, God chooses a king after *His* own heart (1 Sam. 13:14). Young David is without honor even among his own family, but God explains His unlikely choice: "Man looks on the outward appearance, but the LORD looks on the heart" (16:7). But David's road to the kingship is neither quick nor easy. He will be hunted by the jealous and mercurial Saul for the next fifteen years.

When you read David's famous encounter with Goliath (chapter 17), avoid the temptation to see yourself as the heroic David in this story. Here and throughout the Old Testament, we are the cowering, untrusting Israelites. Our weakness shows God's strength. Our helplessness displays God's glory. Jesus is our giant-slayer and we get to rest in His miraculous victory.

As Saul wanes and David grows greater (chapters 18–30), notice how God protects David in the face of Saul's superior force and resources. Marvel at the selflessness of Saul's son Jonathan, who puts his friendship with David before his own future kingship. Admire David's steadfast refusal to raise a hand against Saul, God's anointed king.

PSALMS records the intimate and personal nature of a relationship with God. The psalmists capture how theology impacts real life: how what we believe about God affects how we feel toward Him. The psalms we read this week were written by young David during the parts of his story that we have just read. Despite his unfulfilled desires for justice and peace, David's faith in God's eternal purpose and goodness is unshaken.

David & Goliath   Jonathan

2 SAMUEL begins with the tragic death of

Saul and Jonathan. Civil war ensues as Saul's son Ish-bosheth claims the throne (chapter 2). As David eventually emerges victorious, notice David's continuing attitude of mercy toward those who oppose him, and his loyalty to the memory of Saul.

Once David's rule is consolidated in the new capital, Jerusalem, David aspires to build a permanent temple for God (2 Sam. 7:1-2). Although this is not yet God's will, God blesses David for having his heart in the right place and tells him that his son will be the one to build this temple. And God makes a new covenant: David's descendants will be a permanent dynasty of kings of Israel (7:16). As we keep our eye on God's unfolding promise to restore all things, this is an important revelation. The One promised to Adam and Eve and to Abraham, Isaac, and Jacob will be a king. This Davidic line of kings will culminate with Jesus, the King of kings (Rev. 19:16) who will reign forever! From this point on, we will be looking for this King to come.

Chapters 11 and 12 describe David's great sin—adultery with Bathsheba and the murder of her hus-band—and its consequences. We cannot help but be severely disappointed. Here we thought we had a hero, but even David, the man after God's own heart, falls short, as all men do. This sets our eyes on our need for the greater Hero and greater King to come: Jesus.

Psalm 51 gives us a glimpse into David's broken and humbled heart. This is a poignant psalm of repentance.

David becomes king   The ark of the covenant moved to Jerusalem

David is forgiven and will continue to walk with God; however, he will endure the consequences of his sin for the rest of his life (2 Sam. 12:10).

David's dysfunctional family plunges the nation into civil war yet again, as his son Absalom lays claim to the throne (2 Sam. 13–19). We leave off at a time of uncertainty, but David's psalms from this time remind us that God is ever faithful to those who trust in Him.

David & Bathsheba   Absalom

Key own eye or who God is.

WEEK 5

29 ☐ 2 Samuel 21–24
   ☐ 1 Kings 1
   ☐ Psalms 4–6, 8–9, 11–21

30 ☐ Psalms 22–32, 35–41, 53, 55, 58, 61–62, 64–70, 86, 95, 101, 103, 108–110

31 ☐ Psalms 50, 73–83, 88–89, 122, 124, 131, 133, 138–141, 143–145
   ☐ 1 Kings 2–3

32 ☐ Song of Solomon
   ☐ Proverbs 1–18

33 ☐ Proverbs 19–31
   ☐ 1 Kings 4–7

34 ☐ Psalms 72, 127
   ☐ 1 Kings 8–11
   ☐ Ecclesiastes 1–8

35 ☐ Ecclesiastes 9–12
   ☐ 1 Kings 12–19

Psalms – 3 categories
Hope, lament, praise
Deut 17 – expectations of a king

DON'T MISS >>>

> David is at the end of his life and his son Solomon is preparing to ascend the throne.

> Here we will read much of Psalms and the remainder of the wisdom literature—Song of Solomon, Proverbs, and Ecclesiastes. Consider what these books claim to be the beginning of wisdom.

> Closely watch Solomon. Although he is known as the wisest man to live, do not be afraid to measure his life against God's law. Do you see where he comes up short?

> After Solomon, the kingdom splits. The northern kingdom will be called Israel. The southern kingdom will be called Judah. Both kingdoms are rebellious. God sends prophets . . . prepare to meet Elijah!

←

"The fear of the LORD is the beginning of wisdom.**"**

Proverbs 9:10a

2 SAMUEL closes at the end of David's life,

with his son Solomon poised to become king after him. As we reflect on David's life, what does it mean that he was "a man after God's own heart" (1 Sam. 13:14, Acts 13:22)? After all, we have seen all of David's dirty laundry. He has proven to be an adulterer, a murderer, a weak father, and a prideful ruler.

We must remember that everyone, even David, has fallen short of God's glory and needs a Savior. But David's heart was special. He never turned to worship the false gods of the Canaanites; he pursued God and desired what God wanted. And his heart was repentant (Ps. 51). When David fell, he fell forward at the feet of God. He knew his salvation was entirely a gift of God's grace and mercy. It is for these reasons that, as we read on, all future kings will be compared to David and his undivided heart. May we likewise rejoice in the redemption God offers through Jesus at the cross and follow Him with an undivided heart.

PSALMS continues with more writings of Da-

vid and his contemporaries. David's 75 prayers and songs give us a deeper glimpse into his heart of worship, almost like we are reading pages from his journal. These words, along with others collected over the next century or two, became the hymn book for the Jewish people. They are the songs that Jesus sang; Psalm 22 contains the agonizing words He quoted on the cross.

The **psalms** may be broadly categorized as psalms of hope, lament, or praise. Every human emotion is found in this book.

> The psalms of hope anticipate God's salvation and the reign of the King of kings.
> The psalms of lament demonstrate an appropriate response to suffering. They affirm that mourning the evil in our world and in our own hearts is a right response to brokenness.
> The psalms of praise are a testimony of who God is, what He has done, and what He will do. All honor and glory are His!

These prayers and songs draw our hearts into worship. In their honesty, they teach us that whatever we need to say in prayer, we can. David is showing us how to bring all of life's emotions and circumstances to God, where we find wholeness and healing in His presence. As you read, experience the beauty of worship.

There are also some uncomfortable places in the psalms where David prays awful curses on his enemies. They may feel contrary to Jesus's teaching to love our enemies and pray for them (Matt. 5:44). Remember that David's enemies were enemies of God, unrepentant of their sin with no regard for His glory. David's unmerciful words are the attitude we should have toward the sin in our own lives when we act as enemies of God. But do not forget the great mercy Jesus has for you — "but God shows his love for us in that while we were still sinners, Christ died for us" (Rom. 5:8).

>>> WHAT IS INSPIRATION?

So many human emotions are on display in the books of poetry. In what sense exactly are these books the word of God?

The Bible tells us that "all Scripture is breathed out by God" (2 Tim. 3:16), or as some translations have it, "inspired by God." Jesus, discussing Psalm 110, affirmed that David was speaking "in the Spirit" (Matt. 22:43).

So the Bible's human authors were not merely stenographers taking dictation from God (in most cases). Their humanity and personalities are evident throughout the pages of the Bible. Although the exact mechanism of inspiration is a great mystery, it's clear that God's Holy Spirit directed and influenced human thoughts and feelings to shape the words of God's message.

The beautiful result of God and humans working together points, in a way, to the most glorious union of divine and human: Jesus, fully God and fully man!

---

1 KINGS begins with the reign of Solomon and a high point in Israel's history. Anticipation is building as we recall that David's son will replace the tabernacle

with a magnificent, permanent temple. Rejoice as King Solomon honorably asks for and receives great wisdom (1 Kgs. 3).

SONG OF SOLOMON, along with Solomon's other writings Proverbs and Ecclesiastes, completes the books of poetry and wisdom. Song of Solomon is also known as Song of Songs, which is a superlative way to say this is the best love song ever! On display is one of God's best gifts to humans—passionate love—in a beautiful garden full of poetic imagery. This should take us back to the first marriage in the garden of Eden. God's good design for man and woman has always been to live in a committed, covenantal marriage relationship.

We see that the bride and groom in Song of Solomon have passion and desire only for each other. As you consider the intensity of the love God designed for the marriage relationship, realize that it is only a glimmer of the intensity of the love He has for us!

>>> Jesus fully embodies the wisdom of God that we read about in these ancient writings (see 1 Cor. 1:24). His life and ministry demonstrate the perfect application of these wisdom books.

PROVERBS is a collection of short wise sayings that align with God's law and teach how to do life well. The proverbs deal with very common issues of

life, work, money, and relationships. They are to be read as probabilities, not guaranteed promises.

The banner statement in the book of Proverbs is "The fear of the LORD is the beginning of wisdom" (9:10). To fear the Lord is to maintain a position of humility before God, living life in awe of Him, in awe of the gift of life, and in awe of how He says to live it.

Proverbs gives general guidance about what it looks like to choose to live wisely or to choose to live foolishly. However, as Job taught us, even the wise face disappointment and suffering. And so, we must read on to address the exceptions to the rules of Proverbs.

>>> The five Old Testament books of **poetry and wisdom** are Job, Psalms, Proverbs, Ecclesiastes, and Song of Solomon. Each tackles the question of what it looks like to live wisely in God's world. They all come to the same conclusion: the fear of the Lord is the answer to doing life well. Only when read all together do these books reveal a *complete* picture of the good life.

> In Job, the fear of the Lord gives purpose to suffering.
> In Psalms, the fear of the Lord unlocks God's blessings.
> In Proverbs, the fear of the Lord helps us live well.
> In Ecclesiastes, the fear of the Lord gives meaning to life.
> In Song of Solomon, the fear of the Lord unites us to Him.

→

ECCLESIASTES is a book that contemplates everything "under the sun" and considers the exceptions to the wise life lived according to Proverbs. At first reading, Ecclesiastes comes across as very gloomy, almost depressing. But with further reading, it reveals a deep, reflective look at the meaning of true joy in life.

The key to understanding Ecclesiastes is to realize that the "Preacher" (1:1; in some translations "Teacher") and the author are two different voices. The Preacher is the pessimistic character who deliberates through the bulk of the book. The author introduces the Preacher and then we don't hear from the author again until the end (12:9–14) where he summarizes what the Preacher has discovered.

The Preacher considers all the ways people unwisely try to deal with life by finding meaning and purpose apart from God—education, pleasure, wealth, work. He expresses frustration with the apparent randomness of fate, concluding that man will find fulfillment when he accepts life as it is, receiving and enjoying the simple, good things as gifts from God.

The author finally returns to conclude that we should fear God and follow His commands (12:13). Again, the fear of the Lord is our answer! We may not understand how life goes, but God is constant and always present. His hand is ever on our lives. Enjoy His good gifts and His presence, and know that He will make all things right in the end.

←

1 KINGS resumes as God appoints Solomon to build the temple in Jerusalem (chapters 5–6). Solomon spends seven years building this magnificent edifice decorated with garden images, a tribute to the place where man originally resided with God. The garden images also point forward to God's promise to once again restore all things. Don't miss God's glory filling the temple (chapter 8).

These were great days for Israel. There is peace, the kingdom is united, and most importantly, God's presence is with them. We read with a sense of relief to see God's people finally resting and secure.

But all is not well. The author assumes that the reader is familiar with the Torah's directives to Israelite kings (Deut. 17:16–20). Solomon violates these directives, putting the kingdom in jeopardy. These violations should cause concern for us as readers. Solomon:

> - allies with Egypt and marries the daughter of Pharaoh (1 Kgs. 3:1)
> - imports horses from Egypt (10:28)
> - drafts forced laborers from all Israel (5:13)
> - amasses great wealth (10:14–22)
> - has 700 wives and 300 concubines! (11:3)

Solomon's foreign wives turn his heart away from God to follow other gods (1 Kgs. 11:4). Unlike his father David, his heart has become idolatrous and divided. As a result, God will tear the kingdom away from Solomon's foolish son Rehoboam, and the kingdom will be divided. Don't miss that the monarchy is now two separate kingdoms (11:30–32). It takes careful reading to follow the history of these now-separate kingdoms as they are interwoven through the narrative. The chart on page 62 may help you keep track of the kings and prophets of each kingdom; it can be confusing!

After the divide, the northern kingdom consisting of ten tribes will continue to be known as *Israel*, with its new capital at Samaria. The southern kingdom, consisting of the tribe of Judah (along with Benjamin), will be known as *Judah*, with its capital continuing at Jerusalem.

The newly formed northern kingdom of Israel begins in idolatry, erecting two golden calves for the people to worship (1 Kgs. 12:28). Israel will never again have a good king, nor hold to the covenant. Judah, the tribe of the eternal King (page 44), will have a handful of good kings and at times follow God.

Both kingdoms eventually come to a bitter end. First Israel will be dismantled and scattered by Assyria, never to emerge again. Later Judah will be taken apart in stages by Babylon and its people exiled. Seventy years later, a remnant will return to Jerusalem.

Before and during the fall of both nations, God sends prophets to be His megaphone of warning to His people. The prophets, as watchdogs for the covenant, call the people to return to covenant faithfulness and warn of what will happen if they continue to be unfaithful.

←⎯⎯⎯⎯⎯•⎯⎯⎯⎯⎯⎯⎯⎯⎯⎯⎯⎯⎯⎯⎯⎯

The kingdom divides: Israel & Judah

Prophet >>> Deuteronomy 18:18–22 describes the role of the prophet, a human who God raises up to speak His truth to the people. Prophets relayed God's perspective on current issues, foretold the future, and issued warnings. Jesus is the ultimate prophet; not only does He speak the word of God, but He *is* the Word of God in the flesh (John 1:14).

God uses the prophet Elijah (1 Kgs. 18) to make a fearsome point about Who He is. After withholding rain for over three years—a direct challenge to the rain god Baal—God has Elijah call for a public showdown with the prophets of Baal. It is God who dramatically sends fire from heaven, to the people's awe. Baal is proven to be nothing more than a make-believe superstition.

Why on earth do these people keep turning their hearts to hollow gods, looking for life where there is no life, when it is God Almighty who is calling them to be His children? In the weeks to come we will hear more from God's prophets calling the people to turn from their sin to enjoy life with God.

Ahab & Jezebel   Elijah

WEEK 6

DON'T MISS >>>

> In 2 Kings we read through an index of unfaithful kings. As the king goes, so go the people. This week we will follow the northern kingdom, Israel, to its end, taken captive by Assyria.

> The southern kingdom, Judah, continues with mostly bad kings, but a few good kings. King Hezekiah's reign is a bright spot!

> The psalms you read this week may have been a product of the revival during Hezekiah's reign.

> We dive into the books of the prophets this week. They can be difficult to get through, but press on! The main message of every prophet is a call to be faithful to God.

←

"Yet the LORD warned Israel and Judah
by every prophet and every seer.**"**

2 Kings 17:13a

1 KINGS concludes with the inglorious defeat of
the wicked king Ahab of Israel (chapter 22). It's grue-
some, but it's to fulfill God's promise (21:20–24) to
avenge the evil he and his wife had committed.

2 KINGS begins with the ongoing ministry of
the prophet Elijah and his successor, Elisha. Their miracles are bright lights during a dark time, and they point
us forward to the miracles of Jesus. In turn, Jesus will
point back to Elijah as the quintessential prophet.
Alongside Moses, who represents the law, Elijah appears with Jesus when God affirms that Jesus is the
fulfillment of the law and the prophets (Matt. 17:1–5).

The next century will be a chaotic, evil period, yet God
continues sending His prophets to talk sense to the
people and call them back to Himself. This week we
will read a few books of the minor prophets. They are
called *minor* not because they are any less important,
but because they are short. These twelve books from
Hosea to Malachi all fit onto one traditional Hebrew
Bible scroll.

Elisha

>>> HOW TO MAKE SENSE OF PROPHECY?

The books of prophecy can be difficult for the modern reader. They are often written in dense poetic verse—which is not the way we speak. They are filled with allusions to foreign, ancient things and places—for which we have little context. Most everyone finds them difficult!

The trick is not to get lost in the details. Draw back and try to identify the big themes (usually judgment, mercy, hope, and/or Jesus). Think of the prophets as God's commentators on the history playing out.

Understand that the books of prophecy serve a three-fold purpose:

> They communicate a specific message from God to the people in the age it was written.
> They predict events of near-future judgment, the distant-future coming of the Messiah, or the still-future Messianic kingdom on earth.
> They speak to today's readers concerning the ways of our own hearts.

The goal in reading prophecy is to keep our eyes on and our hearts open to all three levels of meaning: the past, the future, and the now.

JONAH contains a story about the prophet rather than the more typical long-form message from the prophet. In this story, everyone does the opposite of what you would expect. The prophet Jonah is sent to Nineveh—the capital of Assyria, Israel's worst enemy—

and in disobedience he refuses to go. By contrast, the sailors on Jonah's ship, the great fish, and even the people of Nineveh all obey God.

God's unexpected mercy upon that nation, known and feared for its war crimes, reveals the truth that God's heart is for the whole world, *even for our enemies.* Jonah does not respond well to this truth (4:1–3). Do we? Are we willing to be used to extend God's mercy to the whole world, even our enemies?

AMOS was a shepherd and fig farmer who prophesied during the time of Jeroboam II of Israel. This was a time of peace and prosperity, and Israel misunderstood this as God's blessing, assuming the "day of the LORD" would mean judgment on the surrounding enemy nations. Amos has another word for them. Israel and Judah are rotten with religious hypocrisy and social injustice. The day of the Lord will come severely upon them; Israel's exile is looming (5:27) and so is a famine of the word of God (8:11). Yet Amos ends with a promise of restoration for a remnant of God's people (9:11–15).

The day of the Lord >>> when all God's enemies will be judged spectacularly. The ultimate day of the Lord is still to come in the end times (2 Pet. 3:10), but the term is used throughout the books of prophecy to describe imminent times of drastic judgment, such as the utter defeat that befell both Israel and Judah.

More prophets

KINGS & PROPHETS OF THE DIVIDED KINGDOM

>>> ISRAEL	PROPHETS	JUDAH <<<	
Jeroboam I	< Ahijah	Rehoboam	
Nadab	Shemaiah >	Abijam	
Baasha	< Hanani >	Asa	
Elah	< Jehu		< 900 BC
Zimri			
Omri		Jehoshaphat	
Ahab	< Elijah		
Ahaziah	< Micaiah	Jehoram	
Joram (Jehoram)	< Elisha	Ahaziah	
Jehu		Athaliah	
		Joash (Jehoash)	
Jehoahaz			
Jehoash (Joash)			
Jeroboam II	< Jonah	Amaziah	< 800 BC
Zechariah	< Amos >		
Shallum			
Menahem	< Hosea	Azariah (Uzziah)	
Pekahiah			
Pekah	Isaiah >	Jotham	
Hoshea	< Micah >	Ahaz	
	Habakkuk >	Hezekiah ♀ Light	
	Zephaniah >		< 700 BC
		Manasseh	

ISRAEL
> northern kingdom
> capital: Samaria
> no godly kings
> destroyed by Assyria

JUDAH
> southern kingdom
> capital: Jerusalem
> kings descended
  from David
> exiled to Babylon

		Amon	
		Josiah ♀ light	
	Jeremiah >		
		Jehoahaz	is group Daniel tu
		Jehoiakim	2nd
	Ezekiel >	Jehoiachin	< 600 BC
		Zedekiah	

ISAIAH is the first major prophet we meet; his book and those of Jeremiah (including his Lamentations), Ezekiel, and Daniel are *major* because of their great length. Each book is a non-chronological compilation of messages spanning decades of prophetic service.

Isaiah was a statesman and part of the Judean aristocracy. The chapters we read early in this week foretell the doom of the northern kingdom of Israel at the hands of Assyria (chapters 8 and 10). But Isaiah's earliest message (chapter 6) is an astonishing one: Isaiah has a vision of himself in the very presence of God. He fears because he knows he is impure and he will surely die in the presence of God's holiness. However, a heavenly creature takes a coal from the altar and touches Isaiah's lips, and he is purified.

This is a new thing, and a picture of what Jesus would one day do on earth. Normally, Isaiah's impurity would be imparted to the object making it impure — not the other way around. In Jesus's ministry, He was constantly touching the broken, sick, and impure and transferring His healing, wholeness, and purity to them. It's what He came to do — to impart His purity to sinful man — and He does so for all who believe in Him! Look for additional portraits of Jesus in Isaiah 9 and 11.

MICAH was another country prophet, a contemporary of Isaiah who spoke to the common people of Israel and Judah. He recounts their sins, but predicts that after their defeat, they will be gathered again, their enemies overthrown, and the covenant with Abraham

Isaiah's vision

fulfilled. Micah lays out the simplicity of what God requires—doing justice, loving kindness, and walking humbly with God (6:8). It is not about a ritual; it is about relationship! Micah also includes clear prophecy about Jesus, including His birth in Bethlehem (5:2).

HOSEA was a prophet to Israel (which he refers to as Ephraim). God uses Hosea's marriage as a metaphor for God's love for mankind. Hosea is instructed to marry Gomer, a promiscuous woman (1:2). She is not faithful to him, but God has Hosea pursue her, redeem her (3:2), and love her—just as God does with Israel and with us. The rest of the book is full of metaphors illustrating God's faithfulness, compassion, mercy, and forgiveness, in contrast to man's faithlessness. God's love is inexhaustible. His love is not contingent on our faithfulness; His love is because of His faithfulness. The book concludes on a note of hope, drawing a picture of the future eternal kingdom (14:4-7).

JOEL was written following a locust plague, a classic symbol of judgment (chapter 1). Amid the gloom, God pleads with the people to return to Him with all their hearts (2:12-13). Joel points to God's desire for a restored relationship with His people that will culminate in the outpouring of His Spirit (2:28-29). The fulfillment of this prophecy will take place dramatically in Acts 2.

2 KINGS 17-20 shows the northern kingdom of Israel suffering through twelve more unfaithful kings

over 130 years. As the king goes, so go the people. Israel is circling the drain and in its final 30 years, the descent speeds up with six different kings whose reigns are plagued by violence (2 Kgs. 15). Finally, Assyria destroys Israel in 722 BC (2 Kgs. 17:9). The ten tribes of the north are taken into captivity, never to return. The few who linger in the land will intermarry with their captors and become the despised Samaritans we meet in the New Testament.

Meanwhile, the southern kingdom of Judah has a few bright spots in its own violent history. Remember, the King of kings will come from David's royal line that continues only in Judah. Surviving his grandmother Athaliah's coup, the boy king Joash (Jehoash) faithfully restores God's temple (2 Kgs. 12). The next three generations of kings are godly, but the people's idolatry continues and the nations are constantly on the attack.

During the final destruction of Israel, Judah's best king takes the throne: Hezekiah (2 Kgs. 18–20; Isa. 36–39). Unlike the kings of the north, Hezekiah "trusted in the LORD, the God of Israel" (2 Kgs. 18:5). He scoured the idolatry from the land and God blessed his obedience. In a time of crisis, as his country is assailed by the taunting Assyrians, notice how Hezekiah seeks God's will. He listens to the prophet Isaiah and prays that God will save them, "that all the kingdoms of the earth may know that you, O LORD, are God alone" (2 Kgs. 19:19).

God responds and gives a supernatural victory over the Assyrians just as He promised through Isaiah. God has used Assyria to judge and warn His people, but it is now the beginning of the end for that pagan nation. Their king's pride results in his destruction, just as Isaiah foretold. Sadly, good king Hezekiah's life also ends in pride and self-satisfaction (2 Kgs. 20; Isa. 39).

PSALMS continues this week with a selection of

songs whose author is unknown. They may have been written during the religious revival of Hezekiah's reign, and they feature the familiar themes of praise, lament, and hope, with an emphasis on praise. "Blessed is the nation whose God is the LORD, the people whom he has chosen as his heritage!" (Ps. 33:12).

ISAIAH continues with predictions that Babylon

will replace Assyria and other pagan nations as God's tool of judgment (chapters 13–20). Over 100 years later this happens when the people of Judah are taken into exile by Babylon. Coincidentally, the book of Isaiah has 66 chapters and is often compared to a miniature Bible. The first 39 chapters are heavy with themes of judgment, and the last 27 chapters are filled with themes of hope, a bit like the structure of the 66 books of the Bible.

Those last 27 chapters contain more amazing portraits of Jesus. He is the suffering Servant (chapter 53) who takes on the sins of Israel and restores Israel to be "a light for the nations" (49:6) so that the whole world will be saved. God's judgment is coming—as it must—but He gently reminds, "My steadfast love shall not depart from you, and my covenant of peace shall not be removed" (54:10b).

WEEK 7

<<< DON'T MISS

> Get ready for a tumultuous ride this week.
  The southern kingdom of Judah spirals toward
  destruction.

> The prophets continue their warnings about
  the day of the Lord.

> We begin Jeremiah. The seemingly chaotic jumping
  through this book mirrors the chaos of the times.
  Look for the promise of the new covenant in this
  book!

> You will reach the halfway point this week! Celebrate
  all you have accomplished! Now . . . keep reading!

> We watch Judah being dismantled by Babylon
  through three waves of exile. Daniel, Ezekiel, and
  Jeremiah are prophets that experienced the exile
  firsthand.

"But this people has a stubborn and rebellious heart.**"**

Jeremiah 5:23a

ISAIAH 57–66 concludes with words of comfort and hope to God's people. Despite the coming judgment, God will not abandon His promises! His mission is to renew and restore all of creation. These final chapters are filled with beautiful images of the peace, gladness, and glory that will fill the whole earth when Jesus reigns as king at the end of the age.

2 KINGS 21–23 continues following the kings of Judah. (Remember, the northern kingdom of Israel has been wiped out.) Judah should have heeded the judgment of Israel as a warning, but not so in the reign of Hezekiah's wicked son, Manasseh. In reinstating idol worship, sorcery, and child sacrifice, he caused God's people "to do more evil than the nations had done whom the LORD destroyed" (21:9). His son Amon is no better and dies in a coup.

Josiah then becomes king at eight years old. He is the last breath of fresh air that we will have for a while (2 Kgs. 22–23). Josiah discovers a lost Torah scroll while repairing the temple. His repentant response to hearing God's word reveals the humility of his heart and moves God to postpone His judgment for a generation (22:19).

←————————————•————————————•————————————

                    Josiah   Temple refurbished

May we also read God's word with such obedient hearts!

Following the death of Josiah, Judah begins its final descent into destruction. Josiah's son Jehoahaz becomes king and is promptly deposed by the pharaoh of Egypt, who installs another son of Josiah, renamed Jehoiakim (2 Kgs. 23:34). God sends a flurry of prophetic messages during these years to warn the people what is about to happen.

As we spend the rest of this week in the books of prophecy, remember that it is normal to find them difficult to read. In the context of the big story, these often unfamiliar books are reminders of God's faithfulness. If they seem repetitive, remember that this repetition gave the people many gracious chances to repent, and it gives us many opportunities to see God's great love. Feel the weight of the rebellion of the people and the need for a Savior. As the prophets bring messages about sin, judgment, and hope, remember that we are capable of the same sin, deserve the same judgment, and have the same hope. May God's word expose the places in our hearts that need those messages.

NAHUM revisits the people of Nineveh 150 years after Jonah and their revival. This time, God sends not a call to repentance that Jonah preached, but a decree of judgment against the mighty nation of Assyria. The name Nahum means "comfort" and it is meant to be a comfort to Judah that God is destroying her enemies. At the time of this prophecy, the Assyrians sat at

the pinnacle of wealth and power. After God's judgment, they are now just a footnote to world history.

HABAKKUK begins with an honest question by the prophet: why does God allow evil in the world? And how can a good God use the wicked Babylonians (Chaldeans) to judge His people? The answer, as in the book of Job, is not *why* but *Who*. God is sovereign over history and the proper response is to trust and praise Him (3:18). Habakkuk's insight that "the righteous shall live by his faith" (2:4) summarizes the whole Bible to this point and sets the stage for the rest of it. *God judges all evil but he will end all evil*

ZEPHANIAH is a short, direct message of prophecy that may have sparked revival during Hezekiah's reign. It warns of the day of the Lord but promises restoration and purification. It pictures God as a loving Father who disciplines us, His children, but who will "rejoice over you with gladness . . . he will exult over you with loud singing" (3:17).

Discipline >>> God's loving and merciful correction of sin.

JEREMIAH is the longest book in the Bible. Often called the "weeping prophet," Jeremiah was a priest, the son of the high priest who brought God's lost word to King Josiah. By contrast, Jeremiah's messages were not welcomed, and we will see the personal price he pays for his faithfulness to God's call. He prophesies that Jerusalem will be destroyed but that God will return the people to their home after seventy years

(29:10). Jeremiah knows he will not be around to see that hope fulfilled.

The book of Jeremiah uses the word *heart* almost fifty times. Despite Josiah's reforms, the hearts of the people are far from God. Their hearts are rebellious (5:23), stubborn (11:8), hard (17:1), and desperately sick (17:9). Into this darkness God sends a brilliant promise. He will do what the people cannot do for themselves: He will give them a new heart (24:7).

This will be the long-awaited new covenant that will deal with human brokenness once and for all. Finally and permanently, God says, "I will be their God, and they shall be my people. . . . For I will forgive their iniquity, and I will remember their sin no more" (Jer. 31:33–34). In that new covenant—instituted by the death and resurrection of Jesus—we see all the previous covenants fulfilled:

> With Adam — Satan and sin defeated
> With Noah — Human flourishing restored
> With Abraham — All nations blessed
> With Moses — A faithful kingdom of priests
> With David — Jesus forever enthroned

Of course, the new covenant did not come in Jeremiah's lifetime. His persecution at the hands of the wicked leaders of Judah continued as the people tried to evade God's discipline. Though it may be painful, God's goal in discipline is always restoration. He judges His people, but He always restores those who repent. The people of Judah and their final, flailing succession of kings persistently fled God's discipline; let us not do the same (Jer. 7:28).

>>> IS BIBLICAL PROPHECY RELIABLE?

We believe that the Bible is inerrant in its original manuscripts—that it tells the truth and contains no error in what it addresses.

In contrast, Bible critics and skeptics read the amazing fulfillment of the Bible's prophecies and conclude that those predictions must have been written after the fact.

But we believe the Bible is trustworthy on every subject it discusses. That doesn't mean it's definitive in areas it doesn't deal with. And we acknowledge that the Bible uses literary devices such as figurative language and hyperbole. Also, we must not require the Bible to conform to our modern ideas of what a text should be. (Ancient Hebrew and Greek don't even have quotation marks!)

The fulfillment of prophecy is one of the strongest evidences for the reliability of God's word. God wants His people to examine His word for its truth (Deut. 18:22). As you read the prophets, may God grow your faith!

DANIEL begins with the story of a group of young Jewish men who are among the first group exiled to the Babylonian palace during the reign of Jehoiakim. These privileged royal teenagers have their lives turned upside down, but Daniel and his three

---

friends choose to remain faithful to God far from home in their new pagan culture. Though it is easy to think of these stories as being for children, they are relevant to us as we too struggle to live holy lives in a corrupted world. Note the prophecies in chapter 2 that predict the next several hundred years of world history, which will culminate in the establishment of God's eternal kingdom through Jesus.

2 KINGS 24 continues, meanwhile, with the grasping, failed reign of Jehoiakim. His son Jehoiachin briefly reigns and another wave of exiles—10,000 leaders, soldiers, and craftsmen, anyone of economic value—are taken to Babylon. Josiah's third son, renamed Zedekiah, becomes Judah's last king.

30 yrs old

✱EZEKIEL is a priest who is exiled to Babylon, not to the palace like Daniel, but to a refugee camp by the river Chebar. His book contains some spectacular imagery that can be hard to understand. Keep in mind that these strange and memorable visuals would have helped his messages "go viral" among God's scattered people.

Ezekiel's first vision (chapter 1) shows that the glory of God is living, moving, and with the people even in exile. He later (chapters 8–10) sees a vision of what is happening back home in Jerusalem. As the elders worship idols and the women weep for a pagan god, God sends His judgment. And tragically, the glory of the Lord leaves the temple, never to return (10:18).

Daniel in the lions' den   **Second wave of exile**

But God sends the exiles a beautiful message of hope. Just as He promised through Jeremiah, God says He will one day "remove the heart of stone from their flesh and give them a heart of flesh" (11:19). "I will establish my covenant with you, and you shall know that I am the LORD" (16:62).

We too need our hard hearts to be exchanged for a tender heart of flesh: not through our own effort but only through death to self and resurrection in Jesus. May your tender heart be moved by our hope in Jesus and the thrill of what He has done to save us!

New covenant promised

Petra?
People living in
the rules. Edom

WEEK 8

50 ☐ Ezekiel 26–28
   ☐ Obadiah
   ☐ Jeremiah 21, 32–34
   ☐ 2 Kings 25:3–26
   ☐ Jeremiah 52:6–27; 39:2–41:18

51 ☐ Lamentations
   ☐ Jeremiah 42–44
   ☐ Ezekiel 32–36

52 ☐ Ezekiel 37–39
   ☐ Jeremiah 50–51; 52:28–30
   ☐ Psalm 137
   ☐ Daniel 4
   ☐ Ezekiel 40–42

53 ☐ Ezekiel 43–48
   ☐ 2 Kings 25:27–30
   ☐ Jeremiah 52:31–34
   ☐ Daniel 5–9
   ☐ 1 Chronicles 1

54 ☐ 1 Chronicles 2–8
   ☐ 1 Chronicles 9:35–12:40

55 ☐ 1 Chronicles 13–29

56 ☐ 2 Chronicles 1–13

<<< DON'T MISS

> The southern kingdom of Judah finally falls.

> Jeremiah laments the state of Jerusalem and the absence of God's presence.

> Ezekiel ends with a hopeful vision.

> Daniel ends with strange but hopeful visions that lay out Judah's future in the centuries to follow (we will recognize the events as real history that happened!).

> 1 Chronicles is a history book that begins with genealogy. Be amazed at our God who knows everyone by name. Marvel at the plan He had in motion beginning with Adam.

> 2 Chronicles focuses on the splendor of the temple and points us to One greater than the temple, Jesus.

"He cast them out from his presence.**"**

2 Kings 24:20b

EZEKIEL resumes with prophecies of judgment directed toward neighboring nations who were once allies of God's people (chapters 26–28). God's warning for those who do not recognize that their blessings come from Him is unmistakable and timeless. And again a note of hope sounds as God speaks of the new heart and the new spirit He will place within His people (36:26–27).

OBADIAH picks up these themes of judgment and directs them at Edom, the descendants of Esau, Jacob's twin brother. God charges them with cheering on Judah's enemies while they "stood aloof" (verse 11). They will be utterly destroyed for standing against God's people—a warning for all who would do so today.

2 KINGS 25 resumes with the final, brutal siege of Jerusalem during the reign of King Zedekiah. Don't miss the significance of the fall of Jerusalem, the only city in the whole world upon which God has set His holy name. That God would give over the place of His presence—the place where heaven and earth meet!— shows just how far His people have fallen.

←

God warns Zedekiah to surrender to the judgment and receive mercy (Jer. 21), but Zedekiah digs in his heels. As a result, thousands of people die or are exiled, the city and the temple are ruined, and the last thing Zedekiah ever sees is the death of his sons. Only the poorest of the poor are left in the land.

>>> The Bible gives us **three different experiences of exile** through the eyes of Daniel, Ezekiel, and Jeremiah. Daniel departed Jerusalem with the first group of exiles, the elite, who were taken to Babylon. Ezekiel was a priest-in-training taken with the second group to a refugee camp. Jeremiah, another priest-in-training, remained in Jerusalem during the siege and was later taken to Egypt.

To summarize Judah's final years:

607 BC >	First wave of exile (the elite)	2 Kgs. 24:2; Dan. 1:1–4
597 BC >	Second wave of exile (leaders, soldiers, craftsmen)	2 Kgs. 24:14–16
589 BC >	Final siege of Jerusalem	2 Kgs. 25:1–3
586 BC >	Jerusalem destroyed Third wave of exile (the poor)	2 Kgs. 25:11

JEREMIAH, meanwhile, has been in prison

throughout the horrific siege of Jerusalem. During the darkest days of the war, God sends yet another message of hope. He will one day rebuild Israel, forgiving sins (33:8) and sending a descendant of David to judge and rule (33:15)—Jesus. Jerusalem will then be called "The

LORD is our righteousness" (33:16) because it is Jesus's righteousness that makes us right with God (2 Cor. 5:21).

LAMENTATIONS, also written by Jeremiah, is set in the ashes of Jerusalem. These are its funeral dirges, acknowledging that Jerusalem's sin and rebellion brought about her downfall. Lament is the right response to the devastation caused by sin. But lament should always be progressive, leading from sorrow to repentance and then to rejoicing over God's great faithfulness (3:23) which always trumps our unfaithfulness!

JEREMIAH stays behind after the fall of Jerusalem with the new Jewish governor, who is overthrown by a short-lived coup (chapters 40–41). A Jewish commander takes the people, including Jeremiah, to Egypt, contrary to God's instruction (chapters 42–43). The last word we have from Jeremiah is a warning to the people in Egypt who continue their brazen idolatry and will never return to Israel (chapter 44).

EZEKIEL's book continues in Babylon with a series of hopeful messages through God's "watchman" (Ezekiel himself, 33:7) for His people in exile. God's good promises continue with a vision of dry bones that are reconnected and reanimated (chapter 37). This is a picture of what He will do for dead Israel. He will provide all that is needed for them to live again and to walk in His ways.

←————————————————•————————————————

The exile

Ezekiel's final chapters relate a grand vision of a temple that will be built at some point in the future. It is bigger and more elaborate than any temple then or now. Whether literal or symbolic, Ezekiel's new temple shows that God has not forsaken His people. Their relationship with Him will one day be restored to a new and better-than-ever glory and intimacy. The river that flows out from the temple (chapter 47), deepening and bringing life, is a picture of what God's Spirit will accomplish in the life of believers, bringing life and healing to a dying world!

Meanwhile, **Jeremiah 52** and **2 Kings 25** both end with the same seemingly random bit of information: ex-King Jehoiachin has been pardoned in Babylon and will live out his days in peace at the king's table. This is good news! The line of David will continue and there is hope that the Messiah will someday retake the royal throne.

DANIEL 4-9 contains more familiar stories and more strange visions. Marvel as you realize how specifically the prophecy in chapter 7 comes true: the winged lion is Babylon, the bear is Medo-Persia, the winged leopard is Greece, and the horned beast is Rome. Just as we saw Assyria fall to Babylon in week 7, watch a page turn in world history this week as Babylon falls to Medo-Persia (Dan. 5:30–31).

Messiah >>> the promised King and Savior (Dan. 9:25–26); literally means *anointed one* in Hebrew. Translates into Greek as *Christ*.

⟶

Seeing Daniel's prophecies play out in real life must have been encouraging for the Jews who lived through it. God's judgment had put His promises to Abraham on hold. They were not a great nation. They were not in the land. And they were not blessing the nations; they had become just like the nations. But still they had hope. The vision (Dan. 7) of the Ancient of Days (God the Father) and the son of man (Jesus) as sovereign over everything would be the sustaining hope for the faithful remnant of Israel. God's purposes will prevail, and "the saints of the Most High shall receive the kingdom and possess the kingdom forever, forever and ever" (7:18).

1 CHRONICLES will feel familiar since it covers the same period in history as 1 and 2 Samuel. (2 Chronicles will cover the same period as 1 and 2 Kings.) At first glance, 1 and 2 Chronicles may seem unnecessary, but these two books serve an important purpose, and over half of their content is unique. Their name comes from a description by their Latin translator: "the chronicle of the whole sacred history." They may have been written by Ezra the scribe—who we'll meet next week—for the Jews who returned to Jerusalem after seventy years of exile. They returned to a razed city with the temple in ruins. They needed encouragement. To live out God's calling for their lives, they needed to know who they were and where they came from.

Accordingly, 1 Chronicles recaps Israel's history from Adam through King David from a fresh perspective. Extensive genealogies (chapters 1–9) encouraged the

>>> WHAT IS A SCRIBE?

As we begin to read the writings of Ezra the scribe, let's appreciate how God used the Hebrew scribes to preserve and transmit His word through the ages. His choice to work through humans rather than purely miraculous means is one way He has allowed His creation to partner with Him to accomplish His purposes.

Scribes were educated professionals who served as recordkeepers in the palaces of the ancient world. In Israel, they also served an important religious function: conserving and copying the written word of God.

The Hebrew scribes developed an intricate system of reading aloud and counting lines, words, and letters to ensure that no accidents were made in copying God's word. The demand for their work grew after the fall of Jerusalem since copies of the word were needed in the scattered Jewish communities.

Because of the scribes' careful work, modern scholars are confident that over 90 percent of the Old Testament reflects the original manuscripts completely accurately. That's a lot for texts this old—much more than for other ancient literature that modern scholars study. (The other 10 percent contains minor textual variations but nothing that casts doubt onto major events or teachings.)

So even though the parchments and papyruses that held the original manuscripts of the Bible have long since disintegrated, we can read the Bible with confidence that it contains God's true word.

Jews to take their place among the lists of the faithful. If this is not your biological family tree, remember that it is your spiritual family tree if, through Jesus, you have been grafted into God's family (Rom. 11:24).

You may notice that the history retold in the rest of 1 Chronicles paints a rosier picture than you read before. The David story, for example, omits his sin with Bathsheba and his rebellious children. Instead, the focus is on tabernacle worship and on David's preparation for building the temple, the same task that faced the post-exile Jews. God's covenant with David (1 Chr. 17) is central as the Jews continue to await the coming of the eternal King.

2 CHRONICLES recounts the construction of the temple by King Solomon (chapters 2–5) and reaches a high point with the glory of the Lord dramatically filling the temple (5:13; 7:1). The focus on the glorious temple would have encouraged the temple rebuilders of the chronicler's time. This focus also points a modern reader to Jesus, the "One greater than the temple" (Matt. 12:6 NKJV). And when Jesus returns and makes all things new, He Himself will be the temple: the place where God dwells with mankind forever (Rev. 21:22).

←——————————————————————————

Old testament context for new testament
post exile prophets

WEEK 9

57	☐	2 Chronicles 14–27
58	☐	2 Chronicles 28–36
	☐	Ezra 1
59	☐	Ezra 2–4:5; 4:24–5:2
	☐	Haggai
	☐	Zechariah
60	☐	Daniel 10–12
	☐	Esther
	☐	Ezra 5:3–6:22; 4:6–23
	☐	Ezra 7–8

61	☐	Ezra 9–10
	☐	Nehemiah 1–7
	☐	1 Chronicles 9:1–34
62	☐	Nehemiah 8–13
	☐	Psalms 91–94, 96–100, 102, 104–107
63	☐	Psalms 111–121, 123, 125–126, 128–130, 132, 134–136, 146–150
	☐	Malachi

<<< DON'T MISS

> 2 Chronicles will continue to feel like a review of the story you have just read in the books of Samuel and Kings. Let it refresh your memory and see if you notice any differences.

> As was promised in Isaiah, the people of Judah are allowed to return to Jerusalem. Ezra and Nehemiah are the story of the return and the rebuilding.

> Haggai and Zechariah are two prophets cheering these people on in the task before them.

> Esther is the story of Jews who stayed behind in Persia and ultimately flourished.

> Malachi is the last word God gives through an Old Testament prophet . . . then 400 years of silence.

> You will complete the Old Testament this week! What an achievement!

❝We will not neglect the house of our God.**❞**

Nehemiah 10:39b

2 CHRONICLES 14 resumes the recap of

the history of God's people in the early years of the divided monarchy. Remember, the purpose of the books of Chronicles was to encourage the returning exiles. Even though they would be back in the land, conditions would be bleak. They were no longer an independent nation, they had no king, and Jerusalem and the temple lay in ruins. It was discouraging.

So the chronicler focuses on hope for the kingdom through the Davidic dynasty. Thus, we read short biographical sketches of each of the kings of Judah. (The idolatrous, non-Davidic northern kingdom is barely mentioned.) By example, the narratives encourage the people to be faithful to their calling as the covenant people of God. They also caution against relying on political alliances instead of on God.

Be on the lookout for new information about the kings. For example, we get more on Uzziah/Azariah (chapter 26) and on Hezekiah's revival (chapters 29–31). Perhaps the biggest surprise is the evil Manasseh. 2 Kings 21 told us about his great wickedness, but 2 Chronicles 33 shows him humbly coming back to God: a beautiful reminder that no one is beyond God's grace.

← Cyrus — Persian

EZRA _priest_

begins with the same words that end 2 Chronicles: the proclamation of Cyrus, king of Persia, authorizing God's people to return to Jerusalem and rebuild the temple (Ezra 1:1–4). These are exciting words if you know the story so far! You know where God's people are (1:3), what Jeremiah has prophesied (1:1), and why going back to Jerusalem (1:2) is so important. These verses remind you that God is in control. The return is finally happening, exactly as God said.

Cyrus the Great >>> founder of the Persian Empire. Foretold in Isaiah 44:28–45:6, he granted religious liberty to his subjects. There's no evidence that he knew God, but God clearly used him to accomplish His purposes.

The book of Ezra and its sequel, Nehemiah, tell the homecoming adventure of three waves of returning exiles under three leaders: Zerubbabel (Ezra 1–6), Ezra (Ezra 7–10), and Nehemiah (Neh. 1–13). Zerubbabel was a princely governor, a descendant of David. He first rebuilds the altar so that sacrifices and festivals can resume, then he lays the foundations of the temple (Ezra 3). But the people become discouraged and stop their work on the temple (Ezra 4).

HAGGAI _16 yrs after return. 1ax the rebuilding of temple_

is the first of the two prophets from this period who brought a word from God to the discouraged workers. He urged them four times to get back to work rebuilding the temple and promised the blessings of obedience.

A remnant returns to Jerusalem   Zerubbabel

ZECHARIAH also encouraged the rebuilders

to persevere. "Return to me, says the LORD of hosts, and I will return to you" (1:3b). In eight visions of deliverance, Zechariah saw Jerusalem restored to peace and glory. In images of a king on a donkey (9:9), pierced (12:10) and stricken (13:7), we can clearly see Jesus bringing salvation and victory to God's people (9:16).

DANIEL, meanwhile far away in Persia, receives

a final vision from God (chapters 10–12). A terrifying messenger tells him about the kings and kingdoms to come. But as God comforts Daniel, His message of hope is clear. Nations will come and nations will go, but in the end political power is insignificant. "But at that time your people shall be delivered, everyone whose name shall be found written in the book. And many of those who sleep in the dust of the earth shall awake, some to everlasting life, and some to shame and everlasting contempt" (Dan. 12:1b–2). This bold hope of the resurrection, of overcoming evil and death, is a power only found with the one true God through Jesus.

Ezr ~ 6:1

Some exiles did not return

ESTHER gives a snapshot of another communi-

ty of Jews who stayed behind in Persia. It is a story of the divine providence of God (though His name is never mentioned) working through faithful people to accomplish His purposes and fulfill His promises.

The story opens at a party. Soon, the Persian king must find a new queen (Esth. 1). A secretly Jewish orphan girl named Esther wins the royal beauty pageant and is

Queen Esther

See God's hand ever though never mentioned by name - God

crowned (chapter 2). Meanwhile, Haman, a hater of the Jews, devises a plan to eliminate the Jews once and for all (chapter 3). Mordecai, Esther's uncle, discovers the plan and challenges Esther to speak up for her people: "For if you keep silent at this time, relief and deliverance will rise for the Jews from another place, but you and your father's house will perish. And who knows whether you have not come to the kingdom for such a time as this?" (4:14).

Esther finds her boldness and steps up to defend her people (chapters 5–7). Instead of the Jews being destroyed by Haman's wicked plan, Haman is the one destroyed. We see God faithful to all His people as the story ends with another party—the Jews celebrating their preservation, as they still do every year at Purim (chapter 9).

EZRA continues back in Judah as the people, spurred on by God's prophets, resume their work on the temple (chapters 5–6). Notice, though, that although the completion of the temple is a joyous occasion (6:16), the glory of God's presence does not return. The awesome glory of God filling the temple and tabernacle in former days is now sadly absent.

The final chapters of Ezra take place fifty years after the temple has been rebuilt. A new leader is returning to Jerusalem: Ezra, a priest and scribe. He is on a mission to teach the people God's laws (7:10, 25). As his heart breaks over the people's disobedience to God (chapter 9), the people join him in weeping over their sin (10:1).

Temple rebuilt   Ezra

(handwritten margin notes: "Cup Bearer to King - served it" / "What was God to do?" / "to" / "to" / "king" / "trust" / "worthy")

NEHEMIAH picks up the story thirteen years

later. Nehemiah, a Jewish cupbearer to the king of Persia, hears that things are in bad shape back in Jerusalem (1:3). He heads there to rally the people to rebuild Jerusalem's walls (2:17). As in Ezra, God's word makes special mention of the ordinary people who do His work (chapter 3). The work continues despite adversity and the wall is completed (6:15).

Physical reconstruction paves the way for spiritual reconstruction of the people's hearts. Ezra reads the law to the people, and they receive it with joy, repentance, and obedience (chapter 8). The story seems to wrap up with a beautiful prayer summarizing all that God has done for His people (chapter 9), and with the people committing to serve Him (chapter 10). Yet it is not long before the people disobey yet again (chapter 13). Their hearts are as rebellious as ever. Just like these well-intentioned people, *all of us* are desperate for the heart transplant prescribed in Ezekiel 36:26.

PSALMS finally concludes with songs that may

date to Ezra and Nehemiah's restoration of temple worship. Psalms 105 and 106 praise God for His provision and discipline during Israel's history. Psalm 119, the longest psalm, praises Him for His life-giving word. Psalm 136, with its refrain "For his steadfast love endures forever," is an apt summary of what He has done for His people.

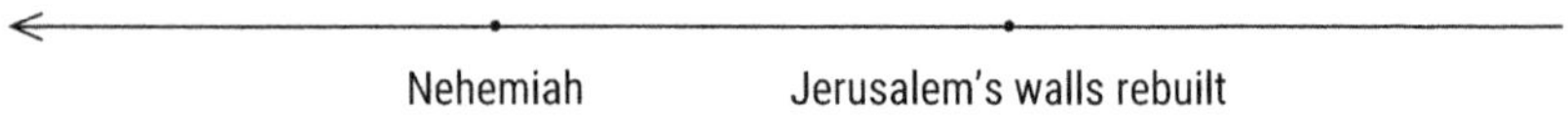

MALACHI, a book of prophecy, gives God's
final Old Testament commentary on the history of Israel. The book is a dialogue between God and His people
in which He lists their sins and they whine in response,
rejecting God's correction yet again. Malachi ends with
a simple command: "Remember the law of my servant
Moses, the statutes and rules that I commanded him at
Horeb for all Israel" (4:4). God also promises that He
will send a messenger (3:1, 4:5) to announce His coming
kingdom, whom we will recognize as John the Baptist
as we begin the New Testament.

>>> And so the Old Testament comes to a close. It isn't a
sad ending or a bad ending; it's no ending at all. God
has said all that He needed to through His prophets,
and His promises are clear. He is determined to restore
His creation and be reconciled with His people. He is
sending a better and eternal kingdom through His Messiah and His Spirit. Salvation and judgment are coming
to all nations.

>>> And so God's faithful people waited, holding on to
these promises through the long years of silence that
Amos foretold . . . .

WHAT HAPPENS BETWEEN THE TESTAMENTS?

As you turn the page from Malachi to Matthew, four
hundred years pass. Knowing what happens during
those years will help you understand why many of the
New Testament Jewish leaders missed Jesus as the
promised Messiah. >>>

---

400 years →

Just as Daniel predicted, Greece conquers Persia, and after the death of Alexander the Great, his kingdom is divided four ways. Jerusalem is then caught between the warring Greek realms of Egypt and Syria.

During these years, Jewish synagogues flourish as local centers of worship, prayer, and Scripture reading for the scattered Jews. But the Syrian (Seleucid) kings outlaw the Jewish religion and defile the temple by making sacrifices to pagan idols on the altar. In response, warrior-priests revolt against the Seleucids and reclaim and re-dedicate the temple. (Their victory is still celebrated annually at Hanukkah.)

As the Jews enjoy home rule, Jewish culture becomes violently divided between the ruling Hasmoneans (later known as the Sadducees), who are more secular, and the Pharisees, who seek a purer obedience to God's law. Rome, having conquered Greece, eventually seizes Jerusalem.

Instead of being a blessing to the nations, the Jews are united in hating Rome. After centuries without a word from God, they are used to taking matters into their own hands. They expect a Messiah who will be a political and military savior to free them from foreign oppression.

But in these "four hundred years of silence" God has been moving! The stage is set with the peace, roads, and language of Rome that will enable the good news about Jesus to spread like wildfire.

←————————————•————————————

400 years of silence

WEEK 10

<<< DON'T MISS

> Welcome to the New Testament! Jesus has come!

> Matthew, Mark, and Luke are three of the four Gospel accounts of Jesus's life and ministry on earth. Each was written to a specific audience with a specific message:

  • Matthew is writing to a Jewish audience to show his readers that Jesus is the Messiah they have been waiting for. He is the fulfillment of all the Old Testament promises.

  • Mark is writing to a Roman audience of persecuted Christians. In a fast-paced telling, he portrays Jesus as the Son of God who has come to serve and suffer for mankind.

  • Luke is writing to a Greek audience detailing Jesus as the perfect man, the Savior of the world.

> Notice the "kingdom" language that Jesus uses. Make note of whom He invites into the kingdom.

Jerusalem under Roman rule

"Repent, for the kingdom of heaven is at hand.**"**

Matthew 4:17b

>>> HE'S FINALLY HERE! <<<

The waiting is over.

The entire story of the world has been moving toward this moment.

The turning point of all of history.

The answer to the question: How can God be both just and merciful?

> Jesus. Messiah. Son of God.

In Jesus's death, God's justice and God's mercy were both satisfied.

> Perfect justice: Jesus suffered the punishment that we all deserve.

> Perfect mercy: Jesus covered all our sins through His blood.

And so we begin to read the good news of Jesus. The New Testament opens with four Gospel narratives of His life, death, and resurrection. Each author carefully chose stories and events that would connect with his particular audience to portray Jesus in a particular light.

← ————————•————————————•————————

Jesus is born   John the Baptist

MATTHEW opens with a genealogy (1:1–17),

which might seem like an odd way to kick off this amazing story, but to the Jews of Matthew's time, it was an exciting fanfare that connected the whole history of Israel to the story of Jesus. As the son of Abraham and David (1:1), Jesus would fulfill both of their covenants, blessing all nations in His kingly reign. Notice the non-Jewish women—Rahab and Ruth—whom Matthew makes a point of including here, as if to point out that God has always been in the business of bringing the nations into His family.

Apostle >>> a title for the twelve closest followers of Jesus (Luke 6:13) plus Paul (Gal. 1:1); literally means *one sent out.*

Matthew was a Jew and one of Jesus's twelve special disciples, or apostles (Matt. 10:2–4). He was a tax collector for the Roman government (9:9), which would have made his fellow Jews resent him as a traitor. Yet Matthew is determined to present Jesus to his people as their rightful king and promised Messiah.

Matthew's Gospel refers to the Old Testament frequently and assumes his readers are familiar with its promises. He repeatedly emphasizes how Jesus fulfills those promises as Messiah and King of the Jews with a unique phrase: "this was to fulfill what was spoken by the prophet" (8:17 and elsewhere).

The message is clear: The kingdom has come because the King has come. Matthew is the only Gospel to tell

---

the story of baby Jesus worshiped as a king (2:1–12). This Gospel contains more of Jesus's teachings than the other three and Matthew makes it a point to show Jesus teaching "as one who had authority" (7:29).

Kingdom >>> anywhere that God rules and reigns. Jesus says repeatedly that the kingdom is "at hand" (Matt. 3:2 and elsewhere). Jesus's ministry on earth was an open invitation to join this kingdom, allowing God to rule and reign in one's life. Those who accept Jesus as their Savior literally become pockets of His kingdom here and now on earth. The consummated kingdom will be fully established when Jesus returns.

Matthew also portrays Jesus as reliving the story of Israel—but perfectly. Just as Israel comes out of Egypt, so does Jesus (2:13–15). Just as the Israelites were tested in the wilderness, so is Jesus—but He does not fail (4:1–11). Just as God gave Israel His law on a mountain, Jesus in the Sermon on the Mount gives a more perfect law (chapters 5–7). That law demonstrates the unexpected, upside-down nature of His kingdom, where the poor, the meek, and the persecuted reign with Jesus.

The kingdom breaks through in people's lives as Jesus heals diseases, casts out demons, and cancels the curse of sin (chapters 8–9). The power of the King makes the unclean clean and makes enemies into friends. But this kingdom is on a collision course with the kingdom of the world. The jealous Jewish leaders begin to conspire against Jesus (chapter 12), and as Matthew's narrative continues, a final conflict becomes unavoidable.

←————————•————————————•——————————

Jesus calls 12 disciples   **Sermon on the Mount**

Of course, God planned it that way all along. In the up-side-down kingdom, the King has to die in order to live. The King must be defeated in order to win. The blood of an innocent must be shed for the guilty: "And with his wounds we are healed" (Isa. 53:5).

Jesus is silent as He is beaten, scourged, and led to the cross (Matt. 27). There He is utterly forsaken as He takes on Himself the sins of the world and God's just judgment for those sins. As darkness falls on the Light of the world, the curtain of the temple, the symbol of separation between God and man, is torn in two from top to bottom (27:51), literally opening the way for all people to come into the presence of God. In this great act of love and surrender, the King has won the victory.

Son of Man >>> Jesus's most-used title for Himself. It is a reference to the prophecy in Daniel 7:13–14 where the "son of man" is given everlasting dominion, glory, and a kingdom of all people and nations. Jesus's Jewish audience was familiar with this prophecy and understood the epic significance of its kingly claim.

The resurrected King gives a three-part commission — "The Great Commission" — to the citizens of the kingdom before He ascends to heaven to be seated on the throne.

> "ALL authority in heaven and on earth has been given to me" (Matt. 28:18) — we have seen Him teach with authority and exercise authority over sin, demons, and disease.

Jesus teaches   Jesus heals

> "Go therefore and make disciples of ALL nations,
> baptizing them in the name of the Father and of the
> Son and of the Holy Spirit" (28:19) — His kingdom
> will be for the whole world, including the Roman
> centurion (8:13) and the Canaanite woman (15:28).

> "Teaching them to observe ALL that I have com-
> manded you" (28:20a) — the way of the kingdom is
> following the way of the King.

Gospel >>> literally, *good news*. This term is used several
ways in the New Testament:

> The books of Matthew, Mark, Luke, and John are the
> four Gospels (see Mark 1:1).

> The angel announcing Jesus's birth to the shep-
> herds brings "good news of great joy" (Luke 2:10).

> Jesus and His disciples preached the "gospel of the
> kingdom" (Matt. 4:23; Mark 16:15; Acts 15:7).

> Paul summarizes "the gospel" as the death, burial,
> and resurrection of Jesus (1 Cor. 15:1–4) and as the
> power of salvation for all who believe (Rom. 1:16).

It's no accident that the Bible uses the same term for all
of these things. There's no separating how Jesus came
and what Jesus taught from how Jesus died and what
that means for us.

Matthew ends just as it began: with the awesome an-
nouncement that God is now literally *with* His people.
Jesus was introduced — "'Behold, the virgin shall con-
ceive and bear a son, and they shall call his name

←——————————•————————————•————————————

Immanuel' (which means, God with us)" (1:23)—in the same way He departed: "And behold, I am with you always, to the end of the age" (28:20b).

MARK, the shortest of the Gospels, emphasizes

the miraculous works of Jesus and portrays Him as a servant who suffered well. Mark, also known as John Mark (Acts 12:12), was not an eyewitness. Rather, he was a close friend of Paul (Acts 12:25; 2 Tim. 4:11) and Peter, who considered Mark his son-in-faith (1 Pet. 5:13). Thus, his Gospel mainly reports the eyewitness accounts of Peter.

Mark wrote mostly for a Roman audience, so he does not refer much to Jewish culture or the Old Testament. And he focuses more on Jesus's miracles than His teachings. This practical focus reflects the common-sense ethos of Rome, where what you can do mattered more than who you are or what you say. Mark's narrative keeps up a fast pace with a minimum of commentary from the author. Notice how often he uses the word "immediately."

Mark introduces Jesus not with a Jewish genealogy, but with a personal testimonial from John the Baptist (Mark 1:1–8). And then he jumps in to the action. In chapters 1 through 8, Mark shows Jesus working in Galilee. Right away He is healing and His fame is spreading (1:28). Everywhere He goes, the people are amazed (2:12). They marvel (5:20) and are overcome with amazement (5:42), utterly astounded (6:51), and astonished beyond measure (7:37).

Jesus raises Lazarus   **Jesus amazes**

The narrative pivots at Mark 8:31 as Jesus begins to march resolutely toward His suffering and death. Jesus is on the move as He teaches about service and suffering: "If anyone would come after me, let him deny himself and take up his cross and follow me" (8:34). "Whoever would be great among you must be your servant, and whoever would be first among you must be slave of all" (10:43b–44). No doubt Mark included these teachings to encourage the Christians in Rome who were then facing dire persecution.

In chapters 11 through 15, Jesus is in Jerusalem, confronting the religious authorities who are seeking to entrap Him (12:12). Mark's abbreviated narrative of Jesus's trial and crucifixion is punctuated by an unlikely testimonial as a Roman centurion realizes, "Truly this man was the Son of God!" (15:39). It is almost as if Mark has been posing a question to his reader all along, a question we all must answer someday: who do *you* say Jesus is?

LUKE is the longest Gospel and was written by a Greek physician for a Greek audience. Dr. Luke was not an eyewitness but rather a companion of Paul (Acts 20:13) who collected eyewitness accounts (Luke 1:2) to compose his Gospel and its sequel, Acts.

Luke is the Gospel that comes closest to our modern sensibilities, which have been so influenced by Greek thought. You will see that Luke tells us the most about the women in Jesus's life, shares the most songs and

← ●

Jesus teaches in parables

poetry, and gives the most scientific detail about Jesus's miracles.

As a non-Jew, Luke presents Jesus as the representative of all mankind and the Savior of the whole world. In all the detail about Jesus's human birth (chapters 1–2), we meet ordinary people chosen by God for an extraordinary task. Zechariah and Elizabeth are old and barren; Mary is an unwed teenage mother; the shepherds are poor and despised. Jesus grows up in a normal way among the normal people that He came to save.

Jesus's genealogy in Luke (3:23–38) portrays Him as both the son of Adam—the original human—and the Son of God. His full humanity and perfect divinity will both be on display as Jesus teaches, heals, and forgives. Jesus's reading from Isaiah 61 as He begins His ministry sums up perfectly His mission:

"The Spirit of the Lord is upon me,
because he has anointed me
to proclaim good news to the poor.
He has sent me to proclaim liberty to the captives
and recovering of sight to the blind,
to set at liberty to those who are oppressed,
to proclaim the year of the Lord's favor.**"**

Luke 4:18–19

Be amazed that the Son of God took on our human flesh in order to rescue us!

>>> HOW DID WE GET THE NEW TESTAMENT?

Similar to how God supernaturally led the Jewish people to collect the various texts that make up the Old Testament, God led the early Christians to discern and collect His word from among the many writings of the church in the first century AD. Unlike the Old Testament, we know a lot about how that process actually unfolded.

The oldest of these texts are the letters that you will read in week 11. The Gospels of Matthew, Mark, and Luke were written next as eyewitness records of Jesus's life and ministry. All of these texts were read (1 Thess. 5:27), copied, and circulated (Col. 4:16) among the local churches, who recognized the divine authority that the texts claimed (1 Cor. 14:37).

By the fourth century AD, churches around the world had independently concluded that 27 of these documents were the word of God. The 27 books all share three features: They were written by an apostle or someone close to the apostles. They were universally accepted as true and genuine by the early church. And they did not contradict other recognized teachings.

But the fourth-century church did not *make* these New Testament texts the word of God. Rather, God used His people to demonstrate what His Spirit had already done.

WEEK 11

71	☐	Luke 7–11
72	☐	Luke 12–18
73	☐	Luke 19–24
74	☐	Acts 1–7
75	☐	Acts 8:1–15:29

76	☐	Galatians
	☐	James
	☐	Acts 15:30–18:4
77	☐	1 Thessalonians
	☐	2 Thessalonians
	☐	Acts 18:5–19:20
	☐	1 Corinthians 1–6

<<< DON'T MISS

> You will finish Luke and begin its sequel, the book of Acts, which details what happened after Jesus ascended to heaven.

> The promised Holy Spirit comes on the scene in a big way. Follow the ways people are changed!

> Watch as the good news of Jesus is unstoppable and spreads all the way to Rome, the capital of the empire.

> Much of the New Testament is a collection of letters written to groups of believers, collectively known as the church, to explain and clarify what Jesus's life, death, and resurrection mean for the those who believe in Him. These letters are so practical and clearly show what the Christian life is all about.

❝You will be my witnesses
 in Jerusalem and in all Judea and Samaria,
 and to the end of the earth.**❞**

Acts 1:8b

LUKE resumes with Jesus continuing to heal and teach. On display is one of Jesus's favorite teaching tools: the parable. We will read many parables that are unique to Luke, and Luke's versions of other parables often contain more detail than Matthew's and Mark's. Most uniquely, Luke often shows us the parables at work, describing the responses of the audience.

> **Parable >>>** an earthly story with a heavenly meaning, always involving a comparison.

Jesus told parables both to reveal truth to those willing to hear it, and to conceal truth from those whose hearts were hard (Luke 8:10). When Jesus doesn't immediately give an explanation of a parable, here are some tips to help you discover His meaning:

> Identify the main characters and who they represent
> Recognize common symbols (father = God, vine = Israel, seed = gospel, harvest = judgment, etc.)
> Don't worry about every tiny detail
> Pay attention to Jesus's commentary and context

←————————•————————————•————————
    Garden of Gethsemane   Jesus's trial

Sometimes Jesus's parables seem to be left open-ended on purpose. When Jesus leaves us to ponder His meaning for ourselves, we should appreciate that He chose to leave us a beautiful opportunity for discovery.

Remember, Luke portrays Jesus as the son of Adam — the perfect Adam. Just as Adam sinned in the garden of Eden, Jesus obeyed in the garden of Gethsemane (Luke 22:39–46). Luke's account of the crucifixion (chapter 23) emphasizes Jesus's innocence and its effect on the people. Pilate recognizes it but ignores it. The people reject it and the soldiers mock it. But the common criminal hanging besides Jesus accepts it and is saved.

In Luke, Jesus's resurrection is heralded by the unlikeliest of witnesses: His female followers (23:55, 24:10). Their culture considered women so unreliable that they were not even allowed to testify in court. Yet here they are entrusted with reporting the best news of all time.

Luke, a non-Jew, concludes his first book with a great appreciation for how God used the Jewish people to usher in His kingdom. He shows Jesus fulfilling the Jewish Scriptures (24:44) and their purpose all along: to extend God's blessings not just to one family but to the whole world (Gen. 22:18), "that repentance for the forgiveness of sins should be proclaimed in his name to all nations, beginning from Jerusalem" (Luke 24:47). We'll see that begin to happen in Luke's sequel.

>>> We'll read the Gospel of John in week 13, since it was written much later than the first three Gospels.

The cross   Jesus dies   The tomb   Jesus rises from the dead

>>> BUT WHO DO YOU SAY THAT I AM?

As we have arrived at the climax of the story, this question hangs in the air for each of us.

As we read the Old Testament, two things became clear. First, man has a heart of rebellion towards God that cannot be fixed with laws and rituals. Second, God loves His image bearers and desires to restore their relationship with Him. He will not give up on His people. He has bound Himself to them in love. Even in the darkest days of rebellion, He sends messages of hope and the promise of restoration.

Now, hope has arrived in Jesus! He is the promised snake crusher, the seed of Abraham, and the king from the line of David. In Him, the mystery of the Old Testament is solved. How can the God who is "merciful and gracious, slow to anger, and abounding in steadfast love and faithfulness . . . forgiving iniquity and transgression and sin" be the God who will "by no means clear the guilty" (Exod. 34:6–7)?

The answer is Jesus. God satisfied His righteous wrath by taking the punishment of sin upon Himself when Jesus died. As God in the flesh, Jesus shed His blood and gave His perfect life on the cross for us. Then His resurrection crushed the power of sin and death and began the restoration of all things. His ascension into heaven secures the victory of the King and His kingdom.

Jesus is the only way back to God. He said, "I am the way, and the truth, and the life. No one comes to the Father except through me" (John 14:6). His claim is exclusive but open to all who are willing to come.

The restoration of our lives can begin the moment we trust in Jesus's perfect sacrifice rather than in our own efforts. Becoming a Christian means acknowledging our rebellion toward God and placing our faith in Jesus's payment on our behalf on the cross. When we decide to follow Jesus, we become a new creation, a citizen of the restored kingdom. He exchanges our heart of stone for a heart of flesh. This is our invitation to become part of God's big story and live eternally!

Becoming a Christian is a decision of faith. Faith is expressed through talking with God, perhaps like this:

God, thank You for loving me so much that you sent Your son Jesus so that all things can be made new. On my own, I am sinful and unable to meet Your standard of holiness, which makes me guilty. Thank You that Jesus paid my debt and took the punishment for my sin by giving His life on the cross, and that in rising from the dead He offers me forgiveness, cleansing, and new life in relationship with You. I receive this gift by faith in Your promises. Help me to live according to the ways of Your kingdom.

As Christians, we live in peace with God as His very own children (1 John 3:1). Having been freed and cleansed, we truly reflect His image as our lives are changed by the power of the Holy Spirit.

>>> **Who do you say that I am?**

ACTS is the sequel to the Gospel of Luke. Note the similarities in the openings of the two books (Luke 1:1–4; Acts 1:1–3). Both are addressed to Theophilus, to whom Luke gives "an orderly account" first of the life of Jesus, and then of the events following His return to heaven, "that you may have certainty concerning the things you have been taught."

Jesus's final commission to His apostles sets the stage for the rest of the book: "But you will receive power when the Holy Spirit has come upon you, and you will be my witnesses in Jerusalem and in all Judea and Samaria, and to the end of the earth" (Acts 1:8). Chapters 1 through 7 take place in Jerusalem and Judea; the action moves to Samaria in chapters 8 and 9; and chapters 10 and beyond see the gospel being preached throughout the western world.

Just as Jesus promised, it is the Holy Spirit who literally empowers the disciples to go and proclaim the good news of God's kingdom. His arrival in Acts 2 as tongues of fire allows Peter's first sermon to be understood in every language and the New Testament church to begin.

Holy Spirit >>> the Third Person of our three-in-one God. He enables:

> Creativity (Gen. 1:2; Exod. 31:3)
> Prophecy (Num. 11:25; Neh. 9:30)
> Leadership (Deut. 34:9; 1 Sam. 16:13)
> Miraculous abilities (Acts 2:4)

←————•————————•————————•——

Jesus appears for 40 days   **Jesus ascends to heaven**   Pentecost

Beginning with the Jewish followers of Jesus, the church explodes as the good news of Jesus literally changes lives. First there's Peter, who goes from timid denier of Jesus to bold proclaimer in the face of adversity (chapters 3–4, 10–12). Then there's Paul (Saul), who goes from persecutor of the church to its greatest missionary and writer (chapters 9, 13–14).

In between, we meet Stephen, the first martyr, who poignantly connects the story of Jesus to the story of Israel (chapters 6–7). His courage is just one instance of the inspiring example set by the persecuted communities of new believers. In the midst of severe adversity, they encouraged each other and provided for each other's needs.

Church >>> literally, *a gathering of citizens*. In Acts, this word begins to refer to gatherings of Christ-followers, citizens of Jesus's heavenly kingdom. The universal church is composed of people all over the world who have a personal relationship with God through Jesus Christ. A local church is an assembly of believers within a community where Christ-followers worship together and encourage, teach, and care for those in their community. The church is not a building or a denomination.

When God makes it unmistakably clear that the gospel is for all (chapter 10), including non-Jews (Gentiles), the church must face its first internal crisis (chapter 15). Some Jewish believers begin teaching that Gentiles must follow the laws and customs of the Jews, including circumcision, in order to be saved. The apostles gather at Jerusalem to decide how to respond, and the answer from the Scriptures is clear: God always intended the Gentiles to become part of His family. And they do not need to become Jewish in order to do so.

>>> **Letters** (or epistles) to the early Christians, which make up most of the New Testament, explain the "how" and "why" of Christian life, as well as the clear truth for believers "now" and the certain hope of what is "not yet."

If you've studied the New Testament before, you may be struck by how quickly we zoom through these letters. We're actually maintaining a steady pace through the Bible, but you may be used to scuba diving in these books. Keep in mind that the letters were first intended to be read quickly to the community, much like you're doing. A lifetime of digging deeper would come later.

GALATIANS is a letter of encouragement

and correction from Paul to the churches that he helped start in Acts 13–14. Paul writes to tell them the message from Jerusalem that Gentile followers of Jesus are not under the Jewish laws of the Old Testament. He makes clear that the gospel message is that we are saved by grace alone, not by obeying the law (Gal. 2:16). Our right standing before God is based only on our faith in the work Jesus did on the cross. There He offered Himself as the fulfillment of every single law that we could never keep on our own. The law was always meant to point us to our need for a Savior, Jesus (3:24). Believe in Him, Paul says, and walk in the freedom He gives!

←————————————————•————————————•————————————

Saul's conversion   John Mark

JAMES, the half-brother of Jesus whom we saw

leading the Jerusalem church in Acts 15, writes a letter of very practical advice to Jewish Christians. In five short chapters, he makes more than fifty direct calls for obedience! One of James's most noteworthy teachings is that faith requires obedience—the mark of saving faith. He makes the strong statement that "faith by itself, if it does not have works, is dead" (2:17). Our works are not *have-to*s, but *how-could-I-not*s in response to what Jesus has done for us. Works are the illustrations of our faith. Just like children's books are illustrated to help tell a story, our lives should show the story of our relationship with Jesus. What story does your life tell?

ACTS 15–19 continues with Paul and his friends

Silas, Timothy, and Luke bringing the gospel to Europe, where it takes root following the conversions of Lydia and the jailer in Philippi (chapter 16). God's kingdom really has "turned the world upside down" (17:6), and it faces opposition from both the Jewish establishment and the Roman authorities. Just as Peter's sermons to Jewish audiences earlier in Acts connected the story of Jesus to God's plans for Israel, Paul's sermon in Acts 17:22–31 puts the gospel into universal terms that Gentiles could relate to.

1 THESSALONIANS is the first letter

from Paul, Silas, and Timothy to the church at Thessalonica that they started in Acts 17. Paul first encourages the church in their faithfulness (chapters 1–2) and com-

Silas   **Paul's missionary travels**   Timothy

pliments the good report he received about them from Timothy (chapter 3). Next, Paul emphasizes God's mandate to live pure and holy lives (chapter 4); the word *sanctification* in 4:3 describes how the Holy Spirit helps us mature, avoid sin, and live for God's glory and purpose. Finally, Paul clears up confusion about "the day of the Lord" (chapter 5).

2 THESSALONIANS follows up on

the first letter. Paul clarifies that Jesus's return is still in the future, and he urges the Thessalonians to stand firm and not be led astray from the truth (chapter 2). Christians are to remain ready for Jesus's return by working diligently, earning a living, and striving to further the kingdom.

1 CORINTHIANS was written by Paul to

the church he planted in Acts 18. Some major problems needed to be addressed in the church at Corinth, a cosmopolitan port city known for its debauchery. Paul learns that the church is divided (1:10–17) and infected by sinful behavior (chapters 5–6). He reminds them that they are literally God's temple now, with the Holy Spirit living within them (3:16; 6:19). Personal holiness is of the utmost importance as we look to glorify God with every aspect of our life. After all, we are living, breathing participants in this big story!

WEEK 12

78 ☐ 1 Corinthians 7–16
   ☐ Acts 19:21–20:6

79 ☐ Romans 1–11

80 ☐ Romans 12–16
   ☐ 2 Corinthians 1–10

81 ☐ 2 Corinthians 11–13
   ☐ Acts 20:7–26:32

82 ☐ Acts 27–28
   ☐ Ephesians
   ☐ Colossians

83 ☐ Philemon
   ☐ Philippians
   ☐ 1 Timothy
   ☐ Titus
   ☐ 2 Timothy

84 ☐ Hebrews

<<< DON'T MISS

> This week we finish reading Paul's letters to churches in southern Europe and modern-day Turkey.

> Most of these letters Paul wrote from jail. You will read the details of why he was imprisoned as you finish Acts.

> As you complete Paul's writings this week, marvel at his dedication to Jesus and the joy he has despite his circumstances.

> Hebrews relies heavily upon the assumption that you have read the Old Testament. Pat yourself on the back, because you have! Make note of all the Old Testament concepts and see how they clearly point to Jesus.

". . . to equip the saints for the work of ministry,
for building up the body of Christ . . .**"**

Ephesians 4:12

1 CORINTHIANS 7–16 concludes with
more troubleshooting by Paul. Although some of the
situations he addresses—like meat sacrificed to idols
(chapter 8) or Greek headcoverings (11:1–16)—may not
be what we experience today, be on the lookout for
timeless principles that are relevant to us.

Chapter 13, the "love chapter" so often heard at wed-
dings, takes on deeper meaning when you read it in its
original context. Here in this book, after so many words
correcting the chaos and brokenness of the Corinthian
church, Paul gives us this incredible description of love.
Is it even possible to love like this? Only if we love the
way Jesus loves us, with a Spirit-fueled love that brings
life and flourishing to relationships. When God's family
is marked by unity and love, it will invite a lost and
broken world to know the love of Jesus.

ROMANS, Paul's greatest letter, written to the
Christians of Rome, is a majestic treatise on the righteousness of God offered to everyone through faith in
Jesus. Paul uses a series of questions and answers to
thoroughly explain the gospel. First, Paul explains the
universal problem of man's sinful nature and separa-

tion from God (chapters 1–2). All people need the salvation offered through Jesus's work on the cross (chapter 3). That salvation comes by no other means but faith placed in Jesus, certainly not obedience to the Old Testament law (chapters 4–5). As a result, we who are saved are no longer slaves to sin (chapters 6–8). Rather, we are given righteousness through faith (chapters 9–11), and we are called to lives of sacrificial service to God and to one another (chapters 12–16). This book contains deep waters in which to spend a lifetime diving deeper and deeper.

2 CORINTHIANS revisits Paul's rocky relationship with the church in Corinth. His first letter was apparently not received well, and Paul followed up with a "painful visit" and a tearful letter, now lost (2 Cor. 2:1–4). Paul now writes with relief and joy that the Corinthians have finally listened to his counsel. This letter shows his love for this church, the occasional messiness of ministry, the importance of correction with truth and love, and the rewarding struggle for reconciliation. Paul's focus on the freedom and hope that the Spirit gives despite all these challenges (3:17–18) is timeless and universal.

ACTS 20–28 concludes with the narrative of Paul's journey to Rome, where he will finally face Caesar. Along the way, he is called on to publicly defend his faith before kings and governors (just as Jesus foretold in Luke 21:12), which he does faithfully (Acts 22–26). Paul winds up under house arrest in Rome, continuing

The church struggles

to teach the gospel while awaiting his trial. Acts is a book without an ending, showing that the Holy Spirit is still at work and that all of us who believe are continuing the story.

EPHESIANS is the first of several letters

Paul writes from prison. He praises the multiethnic church in the pagan city of Ephesus for living out their calling as citizens of God's kingdom (chapters 1–2). All of God's plans to rescue and redeem the world are accomplished in Jesus Christ; look for the phrase "in Christ" used over and over in this letter. Paul reminds his readers that everyone apart from God is dead in sin. Because we are reconciled with God only by the free gift of His grace, no one has special status in His kingdom. Because it is only in Jesus that we are spiritually alive, the ground is level at the foot of the cross. This unity in Jesus is to be demonstrated through love (chapters 3–4). Finally, Paul finishes his letter with practical teaching on what new life in Christ looks like, combatting the occult works and powers of darkness with the full armor of God (chapters 5–6).

The body of Christ >>> the universal church, with Jesus as its head. Made up of diverse members in differing roles, unified in Christ to accomplish His "good works" for His glory (Eph. 2:10, Rom. 12, 1 Cor. 12, Eph. 4, Col. 1).

COLOSSIANS is Paul's letter to a church he

never met in the city of Colossae. Paul and Timothy paint a complete picture of Jesus's deity and authority over creation, the church, and all of human life (chapter 1). Don't miss this magnificent expression of Jesus's eternal existence and purpose of reconciliation! Jesus was not God's Plan B; He was always the way that God would come down to rescue us. His death was necessary to cancel our debt of sin and open the way back to God. Thus, we are to walk in gratitude with Him and not in our old sinful selves (chapters 2–4).

PHILEMON is a short and personal letter

from Paul to his friend Philemon, a leader of the church in Colossae. Philemon's slave Onesimus had run away, but Onesimus met Paul and is now a follower of Jesus. Paul asks Philemon to receive Onesimus back as a brother in Christ and to forgive him rather than inflict the punishment due a runaway slave. This snapshot of reconciliation shows how the gospel changes everything: in Christ there is power to change lives, repair relationships, and challenge cultural norms.

PHILIPPIANS is a hopeful, joyful letter

from prison to the church in Philippi. Realize that Paul has lost all his worldly status and possessions, yet he still asserts his confidence in Jesus and the joy found in this relationship. Knowing Jesus makes life worth living, and makes dying even better (chapter 1)! In one of the Bible's most glorious portraits of Jesus as willingly humbled and then mightily exalted, Paul encourages us to live humbly in unity and love (chapter 2). Because of everything Jesus did for us, we can follow Paul's teaching: "Do not be anxious about anything" (4:6). Rather,

→

trust Him and His good purposes for you. Rejoice in His love and nearness. Pray and lay your requests at His feet. Dwell in the peace He promises, and set your thoughts on what is true about Him.

Saint >>> a common New Testament word meaning anyone who has been made holy by faith in Jesus.

---

1 TIMOTHY is the first letter of two that Paul

writes to Timothy, a young leader in the church at Ephesus whom he considers his "true child in the faith" (1:2). Paul charges Timothy to continue to live out his faith and to teach others to do so. Paul also gives clear instruction regarding roles and responsibilities of men and women in the church. He outlines qualifications for leaders (chapter 3) and expectations for holy living among all members of God's family. Paul's words were meant to encourage and build up these new Christians who have never before "done church." They are learning to live and work as the body of Christ. Paul ends his letter expressing his desire "that they may take hold of that which is truly life" (6:19). Who wouldn't want that?

TITUS is a letter from Paul to the young leader of

a church on the island of Crete. Titus certainly had his work cut out for him since the people of Crete had a notorious reputation for being "liars, evil beasts, lazy gluttons" (1:12). Many of Paul's encouragements echo those he wrote to Timothy, such as the importance of correcting false teachings and of godly Christian living. True acceptance of the gospel, he writes, will produce a lifestyle that reflects Jesus. Don't miss Paul's profound and concise explanation of the gospel in Titus 3:3–7.

2 TIMOTHY is perhaps Paul's final letter before his death. It is a personal farewell to a dear friend, communicating the legacy that Paul wants to pass on and that Timothy is to pass on in turn. Paul urges Timothy to boldly endure suffering for the gospel of Jesus, to hold tight to the truth and preach it boldly. Paul's understanding of the word of God is beautifully summarized in 2 Timothy 3:16–17.

HEBREWS, whose author is unknown, was written to Jewish believers enduring persecution for their faith in Jesus. In suffering, they were tempted to go back to the ritualistic and legalistic ways of their Jewish tradition. Hebrews systematically explains why Jesus is better than the old ways in *every* way.

The author begins with the strong statement that Jesus is the Son of God. God no longer speaks through the prophets; His final word is Jesus. Hebrews seamlessly weaves Jesus into the fabric of the Old Testament, showing how Jesus is the completion and fulfillment of all of Israel's history, traditions, and laws. These connections should be fresh and clear to you, having just read the Old Testament. The beautiful picture of redemption, begun with the family of Abraham, is now offered to the whole world through Jesus.

It is only by faith in Jesus that sinful man can now approach the holy God. Chapter 11 recounts the Old

Testament heroes who also approached God by faith, trusting His promises. Chapter 4 contains a vivid description of the word of God (4:12). Having read this much of the word so far, are you experiencing its "living and active" power in your heart and mind?

>>> HOW DID WE GET THE BIBLE IN ENGLISH?

The Bible was originally written in Hebrew, Aramaic, and Greek, but God's people have always translated the Bible into their own languages. That's because the God of the Bible is the God of language, too. He created the world using language (Gen. 1), He created the diversity of human languages (Gen. 11), and He broke through the barriers of language to announce His kingdom (Acts 2).

Brave men who believed in the power of God's word died to bring us the Bible in English at a time when the Bible was read only in Latin by priests and scholars. John Wycliffe (1300s) and William Tyndale (1500s) produced early English Bibles and were declared heretics by church authorities. Translation and Reformation would go hand in hand as people rediscovered the ability of ordinary folks to understand God's word and experience God's grace.

Translators and publishers have added to the Bible punctuation, capitalization, chapter and verse divisions, section headings, and other helpful reading aids. Rising literacy, the printing press, and electronic media have made the Bible more available worldwide than ever before. May we never take for granted the privilege of being able to read God's word for ourselves!

WEEK 13

<<< DON'T MISS

> You have made it to the last week! Pause and reflect on how God has shown Himself to you in His word.

> This week we end with men who walked closely with Jesus. Peter and John were His apostles and Jude was His half-brother. Listen to the words of these men who knew Jesus well and lived their lives for Him.

> The writings of John, including the Gospel of John, are all here. John's Gospel was written for the entire world. Consider the words of an elderly man convinced that Jesus was the Son of God and Savior.

> Do not miss the significant "I am" statements Jesus makes in John. He is the I AM we read about in the Old Testament. He is the true way back to God and the only thing that will satisfy in this life.

> As you read Revelation, do not fret about the how, when, and where of the very real events described here. Keep your eyes on Jesus! The victory is already His. If you have put your faith in Him, you are His, and you have nothing to worry about. Rather worship as you read about the throne room!

Jerusalem destroyed

" ... so that you may believe that Jesus is the Christ, the Son of God, and that by believing you may have life in his name. **"**

John 20:31b

1 PETER was written by Jesus's disciple Peter, whom Jesus promised to use to build His church (Matt. 16:18). It aptly follows Hebrews's discussion of *why* it's worth enduring persecution with *how* to endure that persecution. In his first letter to Christians in modern-day Turkey, Peter points to the "living hope" and grace that enables them to endure suffering, reminding them that they were chosen for an imperishable inheritance (chapter 1). He finishes with clear and practical instruction on how to live a life that is holy, different from the sinful ways of the world (chapters 2–5). Don't miss how Peter uses language from Deuteronomy in 1 Peter 2:9. Like the nation of Israel, we too have the purpose of proclaiming God's praises and extending the invitation to know Him to a lost and dying world.

2 PETER is a farewell letter written as Peter is in a Roman prison awaiting his execution. He encourages his readers to grow in their faith (chapter 1), to guard against false teachers (chapter 2), and to wait expectantly for the day of the Lord (chapter 3). Peter has never forgotten his moment in God's glory (1:17–18; see

←

Mark 9) and is ready to return there in death, but his selfless final concerns are for his children in the faith.

JUDE

is from another of Jesus's half-brothers. Jude's message, like that of 2 Peter, is to stand firm against opposition to the gospel. His charge to "contend for the faith" against those who would distort it (verse 3) is every bit as relevant today. Jude's final prayer (verses 24–25) contains a beautiful snapshot of the gospel: through Jesus, God has made us blameless—and we will one day stand in His presence with joy!

JOHN

was the last of the Gospels to be written, perhaps fifty years after Jesus ascended to heaven. As you read, keep in mind that these words are from an elderly man reflecting on his personal experience of the Savior. John has outlived most, if not all, of the apostles, who all lost their lives for Jesus's sake. But his belief in Jesus is unshaken, and he longs for his readers to believe too (20:31). The Gospel of John uses the verb *believe* almost 100 times, as if to gently ask, *Will you?*

>>> Matthew, Mark, and Luke overlap quite a bit, but John contains more than 50 percent unique content.

Look for the seven "I am" statements that Jesus makes in the Gospel of John. Jesus's Jewish audience would have understood Him to be making a bold claim of divinity by this reference to God's personal name, "I AM WHO I AM" (Exod. 3:14). Don't miss the significance of each of the "I am" claims for how we find life in Jesus.

John records his Gospel

John uses the words *life* and *live* more than sixty times! John also records seven public miracles that announce to the world that Jesus is the Son of God.

>>> In the Bible, the number *seven* is often used to signify completeness, perfection, or infinity. John's writings are full of sevens, painting a complete portrait of Jesus as the Son of God.

John also makes sure to record Jesus's beautiful prayer for *you* in chapter 17. If you are in Jesus, you are being sanctified by God's truth (17:17). Immersing your life in His word will change you to be like Jesus. Your journey through the Bible in these 90 days is Jesus's prayer for you being answered!

1 JOHN is a letter from John that provides both a majestic view of the gospel and a practical warning against false teaching. John opens by emphasizing his personal experience as an apostle who has heard, seen, and touched Jesus (1:1–3). His goal is to lay out clear truth for his readers who have been confused by lies about Jesus. Some people, posing as followers of Jesus, have been teaching that Jesus is neither fully human nor fully God. After clarifying that Jesus is both human and the Son of God, John helps us understand our need for God and our identity in Jesus. God is light; we must walk in the light and obey His commands (chapter 2). God is love; we only know what love is because He first loved us (chapter 4). God is life; we can have eternal life only through His son Jesus (chapter 5).

←————————————•————————————

John in exile

2 JOHN's brief message to the "dear lady"
(verse 5) contains another warning against false teachings that Jesus was not fully human. Notice his emphasis on *truth*. After complimenting the lady on the faithfulness of her children, John reminds her of the great commandment to love one another.

3 JOHN is a similarly encouraging note to a man
named Gaius, who is dealing with rebellious church members (verses 9–10). John urges Gaius to reject that evil and to continue walking in the truth and supporting those who teach the truth.

REVELATION opens with a promise of
blessing to those who hear God's word (1:3). Often readers come to Revelation with a sense of dread or confusion, but you should read expecting to experience the great blessing God promises.

We have come full circle through the word in thirteen weeks. We began the story with a King, a garden, and a tree. Then we saw the King shedding His blood in another garden and being nailed to a tree. By the end of Revelation, the garden is a city, the tree of life brings healing, and the King is on His throne. All history has been moving toward this goal, and John is inviting you to "come" (22:17) and be a part of it.

Though often mispronounced "Revelations," this is *the* Revelation of Jesus Christ. There is only one revelation, one truth, and one King. The book begins with a famil-

→

iar style of letters—from John, now exiled on Patmos, to seven churches in modern-day Turkey (Rev. 1–3).

The rest of the book is apocalyptic literature, a form that was familiar to ancient readers but is not to us. It is full of spectacular visions and symbolism that describe future events in light of God's view of history. Many of the images you will recognize from the Old Testament; others may seem strange to you as a modern reader. Do not get bogged down in the imagery; John will explain the most important ones for you.

Keep your eyes on Jesus, who is the Lamb who was slain (chapters 5–7 & 14), the ultimate Passover lamb whose blood saves and rescues. He is also the King of kings (chapter 11), the Child (chapter 12), the Warrior on the white horse (chapter 19), and the Beginning and the End. Interspersed among these appearances of Jesus are scenes of judgment and of rescue that demonstrate that all power and authority are His. Satan and evil have no chance.

The whole work of Jesus is restoration: restoring us to a right relationship with God, and in so doing, restoring all creation to even better than its original "very good" condition. We had glimpses of this work during Jesus's earthly ministry as He went around restoring health and life. And we are busy doing this work now, as the church expands God's kingdom, bringing about His reign in hearts and lives. Revelation shows how it will be in the day of the Lord, when Jesus returns and His kingdom is fully redeemed, reconciled, renewed, reclaimed, and restored in the new heavens and new earth. "And he who was seated on the throne said, 'Behold, I am making all things new'" (21:5).

As the story ends (chapters 21–22), look for the connections back to Genesis:

God's kingdom:
Established in creation of heaven and earth >>> Reestablished in the new heavens and new earth

The tree of life:
Planted in Eden >>> Growing in the center of the new creation

The curse of death:
Required by sin >>> Destroyed, no more tears

Fallen humans:
Exiled from God's presence >>> Dwelling with God forever in glory

---

Understanding the story from beginning to end, knowing that Jesus has come to set everything right and is coming again to finish the task, will make your heart echo John's: "Amen. Come, Lord Jesus!" (Rev. 22:20).

>>> C.S. Lewis's renowned and beloved *Chronicles of Narnia* series follows a group of children and their adventures with the lion Aslan, the clear Christ figure in the story. *The Last Battle* is the final book in the series and, reminiscent of Revelation, it ends with the destruction of the old land of Narnia and Aslan welcoming the children into the new, real Narnia. On the last page, Aslan poignantly reminds the children and the reader that the end as we see it is only the *real* beginning:

Their hearts leaped, and a wild hope rose within them . . . .

"The term is over; the holidays have begun. The dream is ended: this is the morning."

And as He spoke, He no longer looked to them like a lion; but the things that began to happen after that were so great and beautiful that I cannot write them. And for us this is the end of all the stories, and we can most truly say that they all lived happily ever after. But for them it was only the beginning of the real story. All their life in this world and all their adventures in Narnia had only been the cover and the title page: now at last they were beginning Chapter One of the Great Story which no one on earth has read: which goes on forever: in which every chapter is better than the one before.

Take this truth to heart: the story in which we have spent the last 90 days is the promise of so much more in eternity with God. We've yet to really live!

"The kingdom of the world has become
    the kingdom of our Lord and of his Christ,
    and he shall reign forever and ever.**"**

Revelation 11:15b

FINAL THOUGHTS

"You make known to me the path of life;
in your presence there is fullness of joy;
at your right hand are pleasures forevermore.**"**

Psalm 16:11

Now what? Keep reading! Become a life-long learner; you will never exhaust the riches of God's living and active word. Immerse yourself in it daily; go back for deeper study; experience it with a community of Christ-followers; read and re-read EVERY WORD. It will keep you close to the heart of God and transform your life.

We would love to hear how reading God's word from cover to cover has impacted your life. Email us your story at everyword90@gmail.com.

DAY 91 RESOURCES

The following books and Internet sources may be useful to you as you come back and explore the Bible more deeply. We can't vouch for the entire content of every resource here, but we have marked with an asterisk sources on which we have especially relied ourselves.

>>> PRINT

Thabiti Anyabwile, *Exalting Jesus in Luke*
An insightful volume in the excellent *Christ-Centered Exposition* series of commentaries.

Lynn Austin, *Chronicles of the Kings* series
Five historical novels set during the reign of King Hezekiah.

Knowing the Bible, published by Crossway
A series of 12-week studies on many books of the Bible.

Anthony J. Carter, *Blood Work: How the Blood of Christ Accomplishes Our Salvation*
A clear and direct review of Jesus's redemptive work.

*Courtney Doctor, *From Garden to Glory: A Bible Study on the Bible's Story*
A 10-week study of the grand narrative of Scripture.

Nancy Guthrie, *Seeing Jesus in the Old Testament* series
Five 10-week studies that cover the entire Old Testament.

Sally Lloyd-Jones, *The Jesus Storybook Bible*
A beautiful Bible story book for children, but equally powerful and essential for adults.

*Henrietta Mears, *What the Bible is All About*
A classic, accessible reference guide to the whole Bible.

ESV Study Bible
NIV

*Alec Motyer, *A Christian's Pocket Guide to Loving the Old Testament*
A short description of the relevance of the Old Testament to God's redemptive plan.

*Robert L. Plummer, *40 Questions about Interpreting the Bible*
Helpful answers to common questions about the Bible.

Thomas Schreiner, *The King in His Beauty: A Biblical Theology of the Old and New Testaments*
A thorough, scholarly overview of the whole Bible.

Jen Wilkin, *Women of the Word: How to Study the Bible with Both Our Hearts and Our Minds*
Teaches an effective method for in-depth personal Bible study.

Andrew Wilson, *Unbreakable: What the Son of God Said about the Word of God*
A very readable explanation of how Jesus validates all of Scripture.

>>> ONLINE

*The Bible Project, thebibleproject.com
Short, engaging videos on every book of the Bible and many other biblical topics, by Tim Mackie and Jon Collins.

Flower Mound Women's Bible Study, jenwilkin.podbean.com
Podcasts and downloadable study guides on various Bible books, by Jen Wilkin.

*Secret Church, radical.net/resources/?type=secret_church
Video teaching with study guides on several in-depth topics, by David Platt. We especially recommend:

- > Secret Church 1: Survey of the Old Testament
- > Secret Church 2: Survey of the New Testament
- > Secret Church 17: Scripture and Authority in an Age of Skepticism

The Bible Recap – One year thru the bible – each day 5 min Podcast.

ACKNOWLEDGEMENTS

To all the 90-day readers over the last six years who have joined in the journey with us and have shared your stories and your lives, it has been an unspeakable joy.

To Marsha Crowe, amazing women's minister and champion of women, we are indebted to you for making space for our idea and cheering us along the way.

To our "expert readers" Annie, Austin, Bobby, Bryant, Carrie, Debbie, Doug, Heather N., Heather T., Mark, Merry Emily, Molly, Randy, Rhonda, Sarah, Scott, and Tom, as we cautiously handed you our first draft, your encouragement and input were invaluable to us for the completion of this project.

Most of all, to the Word made flesh, Jesus, our Savior who has transformed our lives and given us a message to share, may we always be captivated by Your beauty.

ABOUT THE AUTHORS

Susan Goodwin, Jennifer Peterson, and Molly Sawyer are three Christ-followers in the Atlanta area who have been changed by God's great story. They are passionate about making this relevant, life-giving story accessible to all and about sharing its message with others.

SCRIPTURE INDEX

OLD TESTAMENT

NEW TESTAMENT

Physical + spiritual beings **NOTES**
Reading the Bible - getting to know who
God is and who He says I am.
  Relationship
Ps 119
90 days - looking at the big picture.
flourish
Where is God working in my life? Be open -
responsive.
  About God
  About man
How does this fit in the whole redemption plan.
Karma is not the truth.

48590857R00083

Made in the USA
Columbia, SC
09 January 2019